# Conquering Kindergarten

Reading
Mathematics
Science
Social Studies
Writing



Jodene Lynn Smith, M.A.

## Publishing Credits

Corinne Burton, M.A.Ed., *President*; Conni Medina, M.A.Ed., *Managing Editor*; Emily R. Smith, M.A.Ed., *Content Director*; Lynette Ordoñez, *Editor*; Evan Ferrell, *Graphic Designer*; Lubabah Memon, *Assistant Editor*

## Image Credits

pp. 82, 112, 127, 142 Illustrations by Maple Lam; all other images from iStock and/or Shutterstock.

## Standards



**Shell Education**
A division of Teacher Created Materials
5301 Oceanus Drive
Huntington Beach, CA 92649-1030

www.tcmpub.com/shell-education
**ISBN 978-1-4258-1619-3**

# Table of Contents

# Dear Family,

Welcome to *Conquering Kindergarten*. Kindergarten will be an exciting and challenging year for your child. This book is designed to supplement the concepts your child is learning in kindergarten and to strengthen the connection between home and school. The activities in this book are based on today's standards and will help your child develop essential skills in reading, word study, language, writing, mathematics, social studies, and science. It also features fun, yet challenging, critical-thinking activities and games. In addition to the activity sheets in this book, the end of each section also provides engaging extension activities.

Your child should complete one unit per month, including the extension activities. This will allow your child to think about grade-level concepts over a longer period of time. This also ensures that the book can be completed in one school year. Since your child is developing his or her skills, it is important that you work through the activities in this book with him or her.

Keep these tips in mind as you work with your child this year:

- Set aside specific times each week to work on the activities.
- Have your child complete one or two activities each time, rather than an entire unit at one time.
- Keep all practice sessions with your child positive and constructive. If the mood becomes tense or you and your child get frustrated, set the book aside and find another time to practice.
- Read the directions aloud to your child. If your child is having difficulty understanding what to do, work through some of the problems together.
- Play the games with your child. Read the directions and explain the rules to your child. Then, have fun playing and learning together.
- Encourage your child to do his or her best work, and compliment the effort that goes into learning.

Enjoy the time learning with your child during kindergarten. Summer will be here before you know it!

Sincerely,

**The Shell Education Staff**

# Suggested Family Activities

You can extend your child's learning by taking fun family field trips. A wide variety of experiences helps expand and develop a child's vocabulary. Field trips also provide greater context and meaning to his or her learning in school.

## A Trip to a Zoo

Before your trip, create a Zoo Bingo card. Include pictures of a variety of animals you will see at the zoo. Bring the Zoo Bingo card with you. As you spend the day exploring, have your child cross out each animal you come across. When he or she gets bingo, celebrate the accomplishment!

## A Trip to a Museum

Play a family game in the museum. Have your child pick an artifact, piece of art, etc., without telling the other players what it is. The other players then try to guess what the secret item is. Ask for clues that require a yes or no answer. For example, "Does the item have sharp teeth?," or "Is the item made out of clay?" The person who guesses the secret item correctly gets to choose the item in the next room.

## A Trip to a Library

Have your child pick books he or she has never read (or that you have never read to him or her). Look carefully at the covers of the books together. Ask your child what he or she thinks the stories are going to be about based on the covers alone. Then, read the books aloud to your child, and see if his or her guess was correct.

## A Trip to a National Park

The National Park Service has a great program called Junior Rangers. If you go to a local park, check in with the rangers at the visitors center to see what tasks your child can complete to earn a Junior Ranger patch and/or certificate. Your child can also go to the WebRangers site (www.nps.gov/webrangers/) and check out a vacation spot, play games, and earn virtual rewards!

## A Trip to a Monument or Memorial

Ahead of time, look up some interesting stories about the person who is honored by the monument/memorial. Focus on stories about the person's childhood or early accomplishments, as those will be more relatable to your child. As you stand and look at the monument/memorial, tell the stories and ask your child to describe what kind of monument/memorial he or she thinks could be built for him or her someday!

# Suggested Family Activities (cont.)

By discussing the activities in this book, you can enhance your child's learning. But it doesn't have to stop there. The suggestions below provide even more ideas on how to support your child's education.

## General Skills

- Make sure your child gets plenty of sleep. Children this age need between 9–11 hours of sleep each night. Establish a nightly bedtime routine that involves relaxing activities, such as a warm shower or bath or reading a story.
- Help your child become organized and responsible by setting a good example. Have places to keep important things. Make to-do lists of your chores or errands. When your child sees you making time for those things, he or she will recognize that organization and responsibility are important.

## Reading Skills

- Create an alphabet book with your child. Go through old magazines, newspapers, advertisements, etc., to find an image for each letter of the alphabet. Help your child cut out the images and glue them into a book.
- Set a reading time for the entire family at least every other day. Have your child read familiar words or letters. Point to words that he or she may already know (or words that are similar to ones he or she already knows), and have your child sound them out.

## Writing Skills

- Have your child practice writing letters through sensory activities. For example, you could pour an impressionable substance (this could be salt, flour, sugar, pudding, shaving cream, etc.) into a cookie tray and let your child get messy while learning to write letters.
- Supply your child with writing tools that better fit his or her hands to help develop his or her fine motor skills. Normal-length pencils are often too large and are awkward for smaller hands to hold. Golf pencils, broken crayons, and small markers will make writing more comfortable.

## Mathematics Skills

- Help your child practice counting, whenever possible. You can do this in everyday situations such as counting the number of stairs, silverware pieces at the dinner table, etc.
- Involve your child in grocery shopping. Ask him or her to help solve basic mathematical problems. For example, "I have two apples in my hands. You have two apples in yours. How many apples do we have altogether?"

**Directions:** Match the words to the pictures.

mop

top

pop

1 top

2 mop

3 pop

**Directions:** Circle the word for the picture. Write the word.

4

cop hop

______ ______ ______

**Directions:** Match the words to the pictures.

bib big bit

1 big 

2 bib 

3 bit 

**Directions:** Circle the word for the picture. Write the word.

4 

___ ___ ___

bin bid

**Directions:** Read each word. Draw lines between the matching words.

| | |
|---|---|
| the | of |
| of | the |
| and | and |
| a | to |
| to | a |

**Directions:** Draw lines to match the pictures to the prepositions.

1. 
2. 
3. 
4. 
5. 

in

by

on

under

behind

**Directions:** Think about a picnic at the park. Draw notes about the day.

| Who? | Where? |
|---|---|
| | |

| When? | Event 1 |
|---|---|
| | |

| Event 2 |
|---|
| |

UNIT 1

Writing

**Directions:** Write about a picnic. Fill in the checklist.

## Introduction

I had a picnic with ______________________________.

## Events

First, ______________________________.

Then, ______________________________.

## Closing Sentence

______________________________,

and I had so much fun!

### Checklist

- [ ] I have an introduction.
- [ ] I have events.
- [ ] I have a closing.

**Directions:** Solve each problem.

1. Count how many stars in all.

2. Count how many hearts in all.

3. Count how many cookies in all.

4. Count how many animals in all.

5. Count how many books in all.

6. Count how many turtles in all.

UNIT 1

Mathematics

**Directions:** Circle the answer.

1. Will every bunny get a carrot?

yes no

2. Will every boy get a cap?

yes no

3. Will every dog get a bone?

yes no

4. Will every cupcake get a cherry?

yes no

**Directions:** Draw a picture to solve the problem.

There are seven bears. Each bear wears a hat. How many hats are there?

There are ______ hats.

**Directions:** Read the problem. Solve the problem. Circle your answer.

**Problem:** There are nine flowers. Each flower has one leaf. How many leaves are there?

## What Do You Know?

Circle the number of flowers.

1 2 3 4 5

6 7 8 9 10

## What Is Your Plan?

Draw leaves on the flowers.

## Circle the number of leaves.

1 2 3 4 5 6 7 8 9 10

**Directions:** Find out about your family. Draw pictures of your family members below.

## My Family

**Directions:** Follow the steps in this experiment to discover how the weather changes.

## What You Need

an outdoor thermometer

## What to Do

1. Look out the window in the morning.
2. Draw the weather you see. Use the chart below.
3. Put the thermometer outside. Write the temperature in the chart.
4. Repeat in the afternoon.

| Morning Weather | Morning Temperature | Afternoon Weather | Afternoon Temperature |
|---|---|---|---|
| | | | |

5. How did the weather change between the morning and the afternoon?

_______________________________________________

_______________________________________________

**Directions:** Read the clues. Write the name of each person.

## Clues

- The youngest daughter is Mary.
- The mother is Madison.
- The oldest daughter is Morgan.
- The grandmother is May.

1. 
______________________

______________________

2. 
______________________

______________________

3. 
______________________

______________________

4. 
______________________

______________________

**Directions:** Go on a scavenger hunt at home. Find the things on the list. Mark an *X* in the box when you find each thing. If you can, take a picture of it.

1. the number 6 ☐
2. something that starts with *t* ☐
3. a circle ☐
4. the letter *b* ☐
5. something you can take apart ☐
6. something cold ☐
7. the word *and* ☐
8. four of the same item ☐

 

## High-Frequency Words Activity

Review the high-frequency words on page 9. Give your child magazines, newspapers, catalogues, or other types of printed text. Have your child circle or highlight the high-frequency words in these texts.

## Writing Activity

Go on a real picnic with your child. You can go to the park, your backyard, or even the living room floor. Then, have your child write about what happened on the picnic.

## Mathematics Activity

Help your child collect objects to practice counting. Have your child point to each object as he or she counts it.

## Social Studies Activity

Have your child talk to as many people in your family tree as possible. Have your child ask them what life was like when they were children.

## Science Activity

Have your child draw the weather for one week. Ask your child what patterns he or she sees.

## Critical-Thinking Activity

Have your child work with a partner to make a critical-thinking puzzle like the one on page 19. Have your child write clues about the boys in a family.

## Listening-and-Speaking Activity

Have your child name all the people in your family. Ask your child to explain how they are each related to him or her.

**Directions:** Match the words to the pictures.

|  |  |  |
|---|---|---|
| jog | pop | mom |

1. pop 
2. jog 
3. mom 

**Directions:** Circle the word for the picture. Write the word.

4. 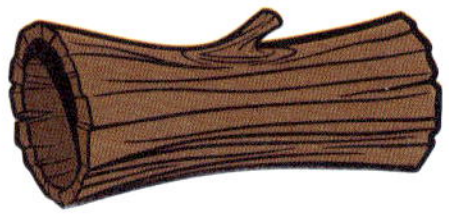

rot log

___ ___ ___

 

**Directions:** Match the words to the pictures.

Ken

vet

10

ten

1 ten

10

2 vet

3 Ken

**Directions:** Circle the word for the picture. Write the word.

4

bed pep

____ ____ ____

**Directions:** Read and trace each word. Write each word using fancy letters. You can write it *curly*, skinny, or wide.

| Normal | Fancy |
|---|---|
| in | |
| is | |
| you | |
| that | |
| it | |

**Directions:** Choose the word with a capital letter. Write it on the line.

1 ____________ dog is fast.
(**The** or **the**)

2 ____________ pan is hot.
(**A** or **a**)

3 ____________ go to bed.
(**we** or **We**)

4 ____________ you go?
(**can** or **Can**)

5 ____________ have a dog.
(**I** or **i**)

**Directions:** Trace the words that are about police officers.

car

hat

police
officer

lollipop

badge

**Directions:** Write about police officers. Fill in the checklist.

## Topic

Police officers ______________________.

(**save** or **help**)

## Detail

They ______________________

______________________.

## Closing

Police officers are ______________________.

(**kind** or **brave**)

### ☑ Checklist

- ☐ I have a topic sentence.
- ☐ I have a detail.
- ☐ I have a closing.

**Directions:** Solve each problem.

1. Draw 1 string on the kite.

2. Draw 2 legs on the person.

3. Color 3 blocks.

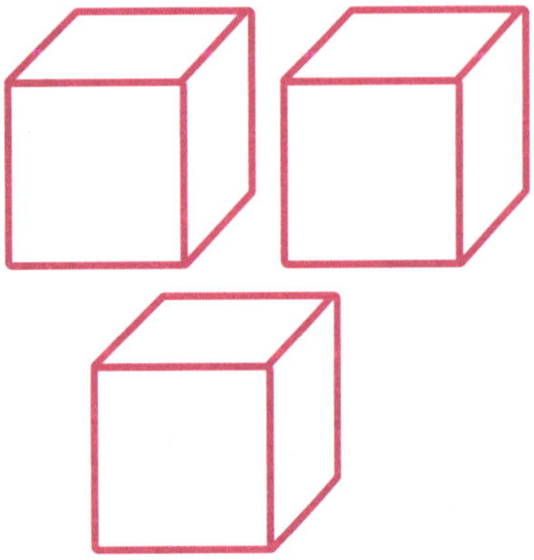

4. Color 4 apples.

5. Draw more circles to make a set of 5.

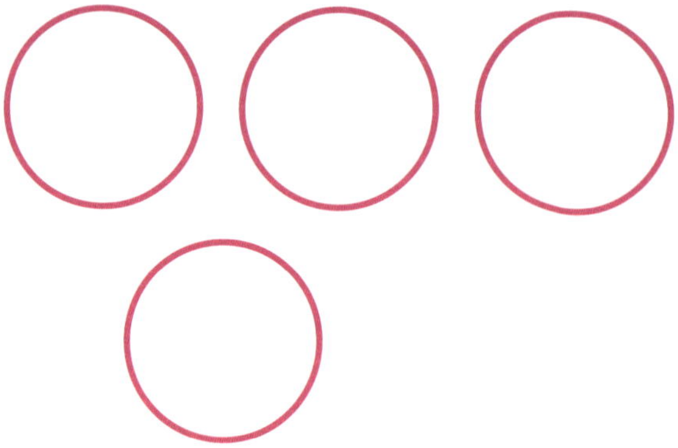

6. Draw 6 legs on the bug.

**Directions:** Solve each problem.

1. Circle the name of the shapes.

rectangles pentagons circles

2. Circle the name of the shapes.

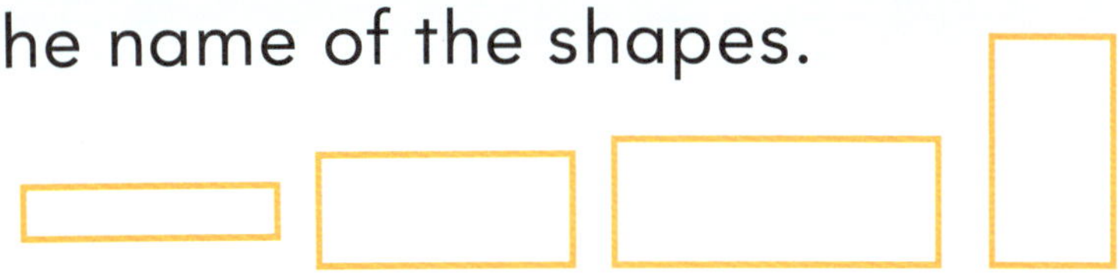

squares rectangles hexagons

3. Circle the name of the shapes.

triangles circles squares

4. Circle the name of the shapes.

squares triangles pentagons

5. Draw an oval. Then, draw a rectangle to the right of the oval.

**Directions:** Look at the example. Draw lines to solve the problem. Circle your answer.

**Example:** Which group has more?

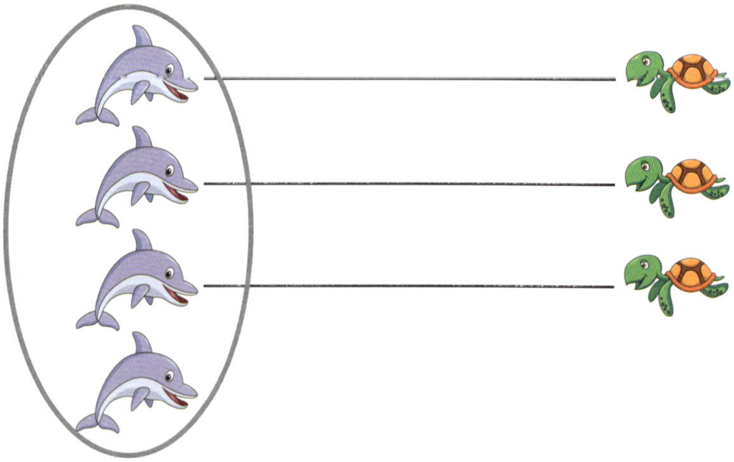

4 is greater than 3.

Which group has more?

______ ______

______ is greater than ______.

 

**Directions:** Draw a picture to show the problem. Write your answer.

Ken has 2 apples. Rick has 4 apples. Who has more apples?

Ken

Rick

____________________

____________________ has more apples.

**Directions:** Draw lines to match the workers with the goods or services they provide.

1 

2 

3 

4 

**Directions:** Follow the steps in this experiment to see how you push, pull, and twist.

## What You Need

plastic screw-top containers

## What to Do

1. Stand facing a partner, toe to toe. Gently push each other on the shoulder. What happens?

2. What happens when you gently pull each other?

3. Twist the screw-top container. What happens?

4. Try pushing, pulling, and twisting some things around the room. Draw what happens on a sheet of paper.

**Directions:** Put an X on the shape that does not belong in each set. Tell a partner what is the same about the rest of the set.

1

2

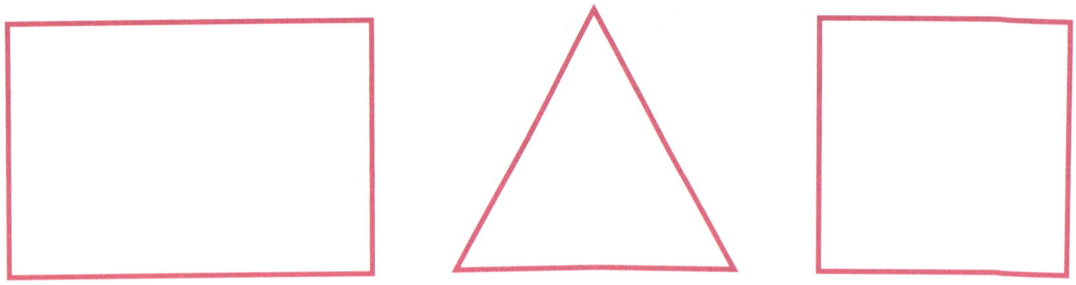

3

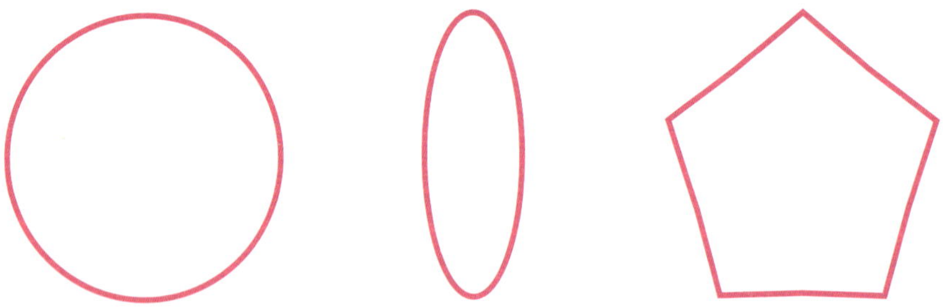

4

**Directions:** Play with a partner. Follow the steps.

1. Draw these shapes each on a slip of paper: circle, triangle, square, rectangle, oval, diamond, pentagon, and hexagon.
2. Put the slips into a jar.
3. Sit back to back. Choose a slip of paper without looking.
4. Tell your partner how to draw the shape without saying its name. For example, *This shape has 4 sides. The sides are all equal.*
5. Your partner should draw what he or she hears.
6. Switch roles. Now, your partner should choose a shape, and you should draw. Play until all shapes have been drawn.

## High-Frequency Words Activity

Fill a zip-top bag with a few tablespoons of colored hair gel or paint. Squeeze out all the air, and lay the bag flat on a table. Have your child practice writing the high-frequency words from page 24 on the bag.

## Writing Activity

Have your child review his or her writing from page 27. Have him or her circle the first letter of each sentence to make sure it begins with a capital letter.

## Mathematics Activity

Help your child make a list of shapes. Include pictures and the names of the shapes. Then, have your child go on a shape hunt around your house. Have him or her put a tally mark next to the picture of the shape each time a shape is found.

## Social Studies Activity

Help your child talk to a community worker. Have your child ask the worker about his or her job.

## Science Activity

Talk about the experiment from page 33 with your child. Ask him or her which things were hard to push, pull, and twist. Ask your child how these things are similar to and different from each other.

## Listening-and-Speaking Activity

Ask your child whether he or she would like to be a police officer. Ask him or her to explain why or why not.

**Directions:** Match each words to the pictures.

mug

hut

tug

1 hut

2 mug

3 tug

**Directions:** Circle the word for the picture. Write the word.

4

cup nut

______ ______ ______

**Directions:** Match the words to the pictures.

tap

tip

top

1 top 

2 tap 

3 tip 

**Directions:** Circle the word for the picture. Write the word.

4

tag tan

**Directions:** Circle the correct spelling of the word. Trace over the word with a crayon.

1. this

this thes tis

2. he

he hi hee

3. was

wuz waz was

4. for

fore for fur

5. on

on un onn

**Directions:** Draw one more picture in each category.

## Fruit

## Animals

## Clothes

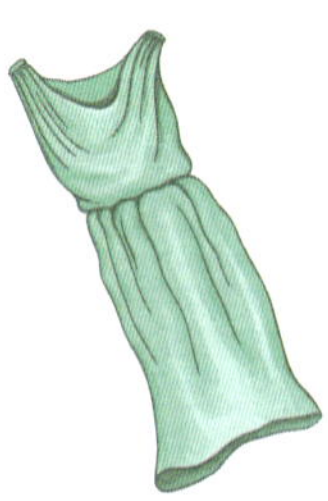

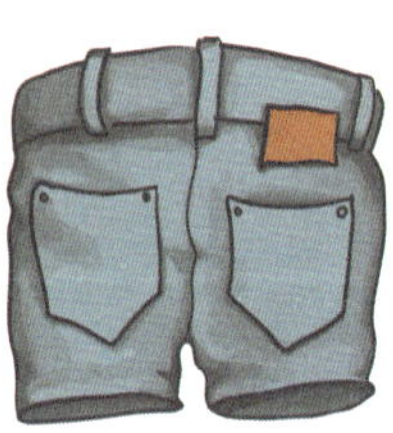

## Sports

**Directions:** Circle the picture you like best. Write your opinion. Write a reason.

summer

winter

## Opinion

I like ______________________________.

## Reason

I like it because ______________________________
______________________________
______________________________.

UNIT 3

Writing

**Directions:** Write about summer or winter. Fill in the checklist.

## Opinion

______________________ is the best season.

(**Summer** or **Winter**)

## Reason

I like it because ______________________

______________________.

## Closing

I love ______________________!

(**summer** or **winter**)

## ☑ Checklist

- ☐ I state my opinion.
- ☐ I have a reason.
- ☐ I have a closing.

**Directions:** Write which number comes next.

1. 7 8 9 ____
2. 12 13 14 ____
3. 9 10 11 ____
4. 14 15 16 ____
5. 11 12 13 ____
6. 16 17 18 ____

**Directions:** Solve each problem.

1. How many penguins are there?

2. How many monkeys are there?

3. How many dots are there?

4. How many socks are there?

5. How many spiders are there?

6. How many carrots are there?

**Directions:** Draw a picture to solve the problem.

Kenny picks 7 flowers. He picks 1 more. How many flowers does he have now?

Kenny has ______ flowers now.

**Directions:** Read the problem. Solve the problem. Circle your answer.

**Problem:** Tom has 4 blocks. Sue gives him 1 more. How many blocks does Tom have now?

## What Do You Know?

Draw a picture to show the problem.

## What Is Your Plan?

Count the blocks.

## Circle the number of blocks.

1 2 3 4 5 6 7 8 9 10

**Directions:** Draw a picture to show what each person has the authority to do.

| | |
|---|---|
| 1  crossing guard | |
| 2  teacher | |
| 3  police officer | |
| 4  parent | |

**Directions:** Follow the steps in this experiment to discover how seeds are different.

## What You Need

- lots of different seeds
- jar with lid

## What to Do

1. Put all the seeds in a jar.
2. Choose a seed. Take it out, and look at it carefully.
3. Draw a picture of your seed below.
4. Put the seed back into the jar. Shake the seeds.
5. Try to find your seed again. How do you know it's the same seed?

**Directions:** Draw a picture of a food that begins with each letter listed.

1. B
2. N
3. S
4. P
5. G
6. L
7. C
8. D

**Directions:** Play with a partner. Place a paper clip over the X. Place a pencil in the middle of the paper clip to make a spinner. Take turns flicking the spinner. Count out the number of beans or other counters that matches your spin. Keep playing until someone has at least 20 counters.

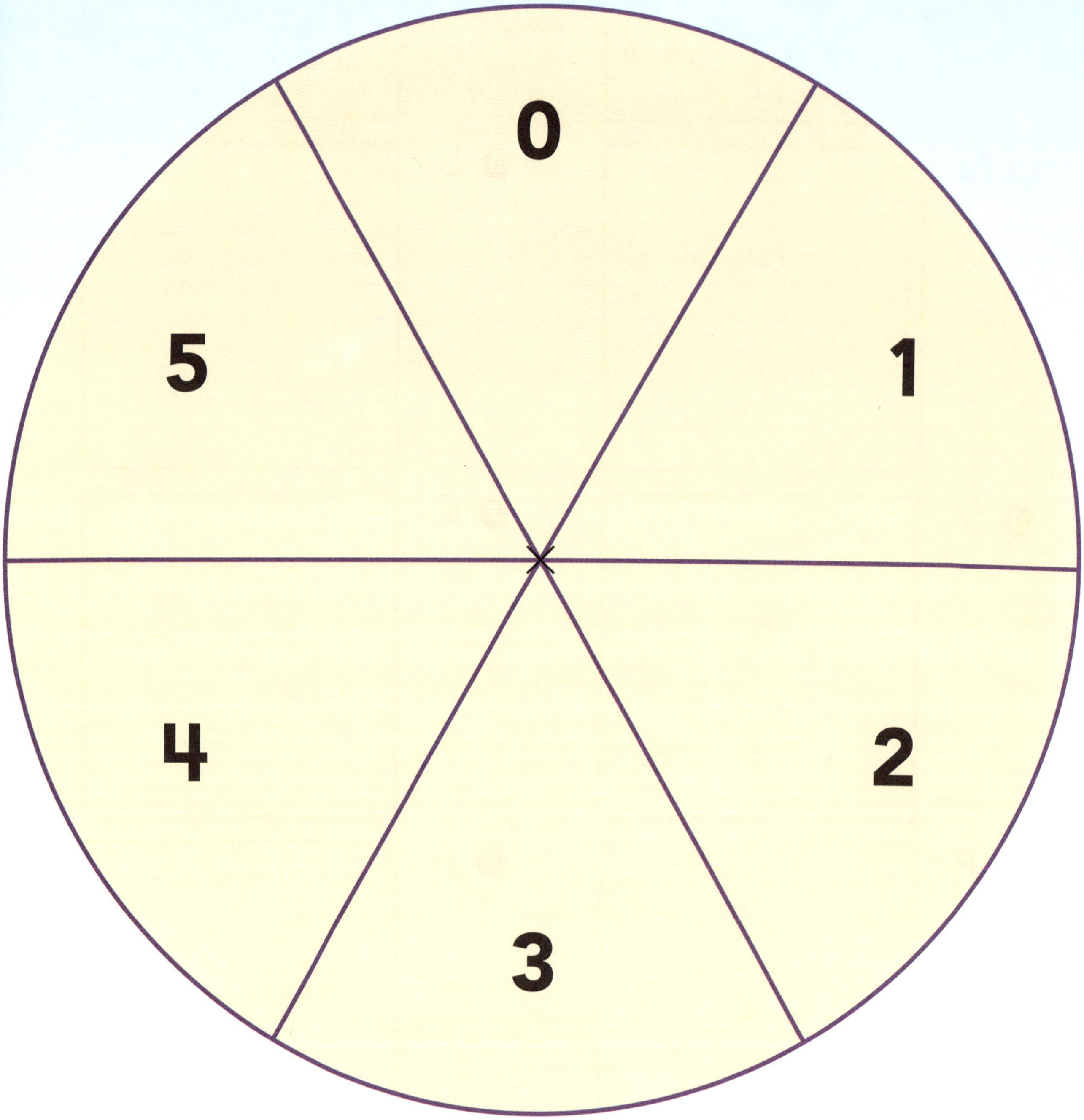

## High-Frequency Words Activity

Review the high-frequency words on page 39 with your child. Cut out the letters for the words from advertisements, catalogs, or packages. Have your child glue the letters on a sheet of paper to spell each word.

## Writing Activity

Ask your child to think of one more reason he or she likes summer or winter. Have your child write his or her reason on a sheet of paper. Or write your child's reason in large printing, and have him or her trace over your letters.

## Mathematics Activity

Practice counting objects with your child while you are driving. Decide on an object, such as stop signs. Work together to count the number of objects you see while driving around town.

## Social Studies Activity

Have your child draw a picture of another person who has authority in the community.

## Critical-Thinking Activity

Ask your child to name foods that begin with other letters of the alphabet. Or, select a different category, such as clothing or games.

## Listening-and-Speaking Activity

Ask your child to name the authority figures in his or her life. Ask your child to explain why those people are important.

**Directions:** Match the words to the pictures.

bat bit bet

❶ bat

❷ bet

❸ bit

**Directions:** Circle the word for the picture. Write the word.

❹

Ben bug

**Directions:** Match the words to the pictures.

cat

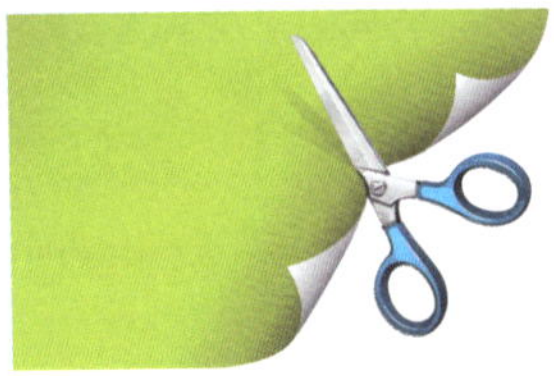

cut

cot

1 cot

2 cut

3 cat

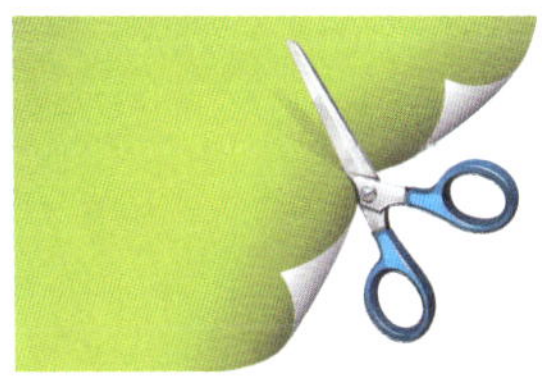

**Directions:** Circle the word for the picture. Write the word.

4

can cap

______ ______ ______

**Directions:** Read the words in the box. Find the hidden words. Circle the hidden words.

| are | have | with | his | they |
|---|---|---|---|---|

1. l r a t i a r e m e s a
2. h w i t h w t s k l m t
3. y e c s l h y a t h e y
4. p m r s i h a v e n p a
5. r s a h v h i s h s e s

**Directions:** Write the opposite of each word. Use the words in the box to help you.

| go | big | top | hot | up |
|---|---|---|---|---|

1. 
down

2. 
cold

3. 
little

4. 

stop

5. 
bottom

**Directions:** Think about a time you did something with your friends. Draw notes about the day.

| Who? | Where? |
|---|---|
| | |

| When? | Event 1 |
|---|---|
| | |

| Event 2 |
|---|
| |

**Directions:** Write about a day with your friends. Fill in the checklist.

## Introduction

I spent a day with ____________________.

## Events

First, ____________________.

Then, ____________________.

## Closing Sentence

____________________,

and I had a great day!

### ☑ Checklist

- ☐ I have an introduction.
- ☐ I have events.
- ☐ I have a closing.

**Directions:** Solve each problem.

1. Circle the group that has more fish.

3. Put an X on the group that has more.

2. Circle the box with fewer flowers.

4. Circle the bowl that has more fish.

**Directions:** Solve each problem.

1. How many pumpkins are there?

9 10 11

2. Circle the machine with 11 pieces of gum.

3. How many ants are there?

18 19 20

4. Circle 16 fish.

**Directions:** Look at the example. Solve the problem.

**Example:** Circle the shape that has more circle faces.

**cone** 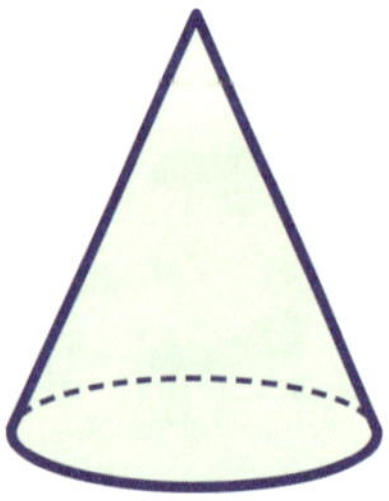

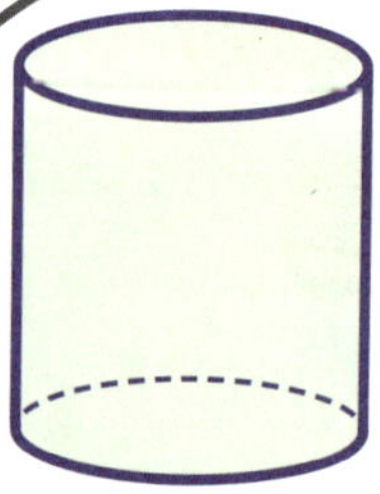 **cylinder**

A cone has 1 circle face.

A cylinder has 2 circle faces.

Circle the shape that has more faces.

**cube** 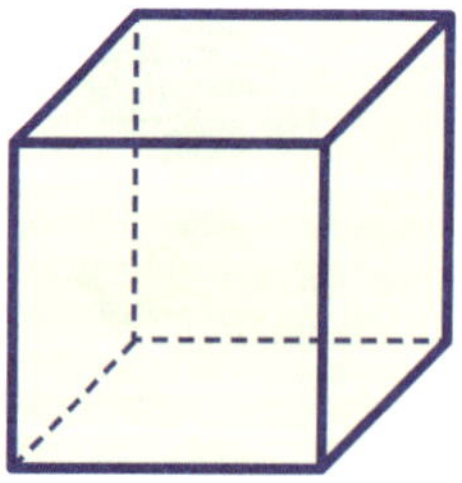

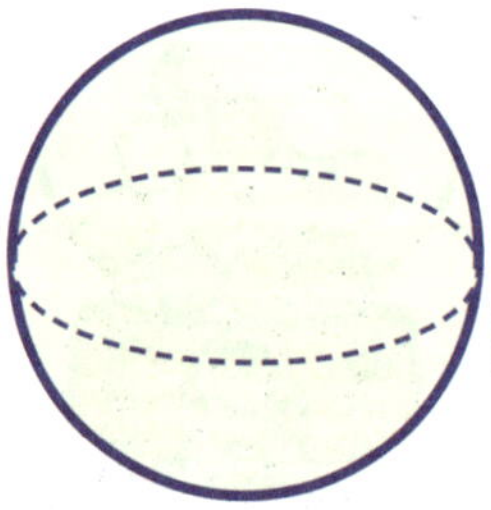 **sphere**

a cube has ______ faces

a sphere has ______ faces

**Directions:** Trace the pictures to solve each problem.

How many corners do these shapes have? Circle the corners

1 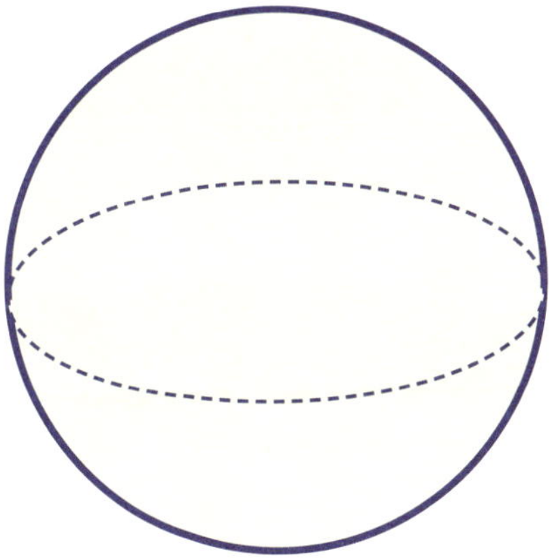

______ corners

2 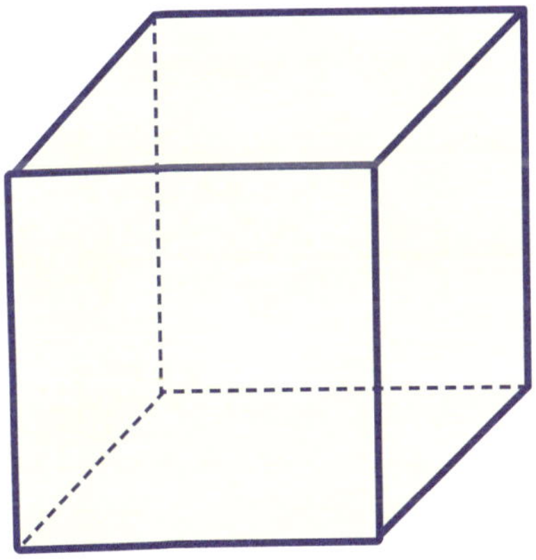

______ corners

3 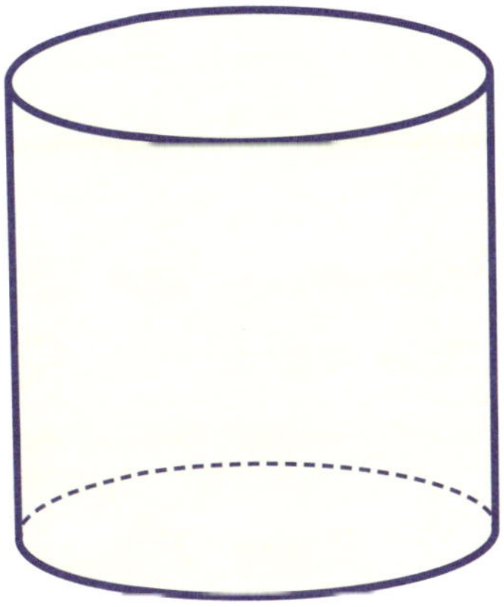

______ corners

**Directions:** Make a time line of your day. Draw what you do during each part of the day.

# My Day

| Morning |
| --- |
| Noon |
| Evening |
| Night |

**Directions:** Follow the steps in this experiment to discover how balls move.

## What You Need

balls of different sizes

## What to Do

1. Choose one ball. Think about the different ways you make balls move in the games you play.
2. See what happens when you:
    - flick it with a finger
    - roll it
    - throw it underarm
    - bounce it
    - pat it
3. Pick another ball. Move this ball in the same ways. Think about how this ball moves.

**Directions:** Find objects that look like the ones shown. Answer *yes* or *no* for each question.

| Shape | Will it stack?  | Will it slide? 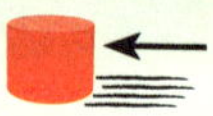 | Will it roll?  |
|---|---|---|---|
| 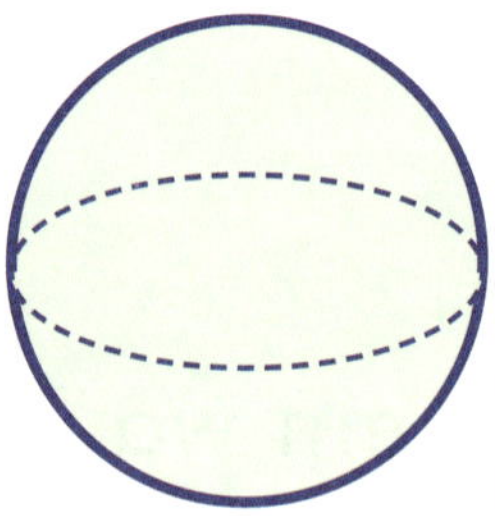 | | | |
| 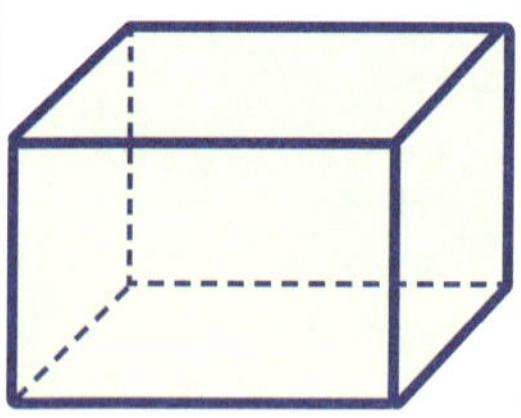 | | | |
| 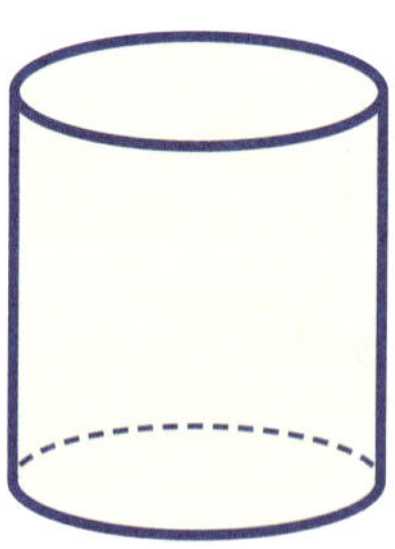 | | | |
| 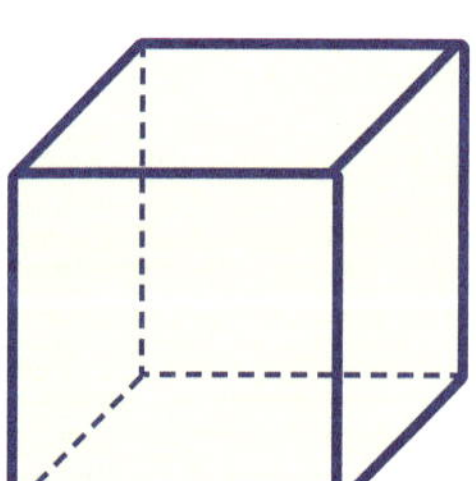 | | | |

**Directions:** Place a paper clip over the X. Place a pencil through the paper clip to make a spinner. Play with a partner. Each player rolls a ball. Spin the spinner. If your ball matches your spin, you get a point. Reroll the balls, but let the second player spin this time. Tally your points in the chart. The first person to get 10 points wins.

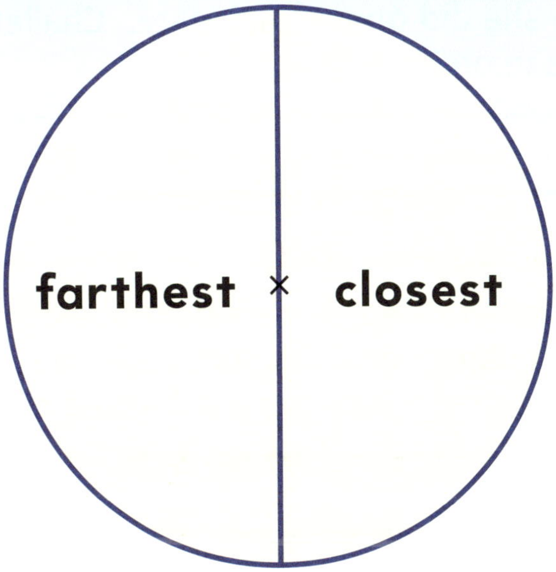


**Player 1:** ______________________

**Player 2:** ______________________

## High-Frequency Words Activity

Have your child form letters with modeling clay to spell the high-frequency words on page 54.

## Writing Activity

Arrange a play date for your child and a friend. Then, ask your child what he or she did on the play date. Challenge your child to list the events in order.

## Problem-Solving Activity

Help your child gather three-dimensional objects. Shine a flashlight on each object, and ask your child to look at its shadow. Ask your child what shape is formed by each shadow.

## Science Activity

Talk to your child about the experiment on page 63. Ask your child to compare how the two different balls moved. What was the same? What was different?

## Critical-Thinking Activity

Show your child a cone-shaped object. Ask him or her whether it will stack, slide, or roll.

## Listening-and-Speaking Activity

Ask your child how a time line for his or her day would be different during the week and during the weekend.

**Directions:** Match the words to the pictures.

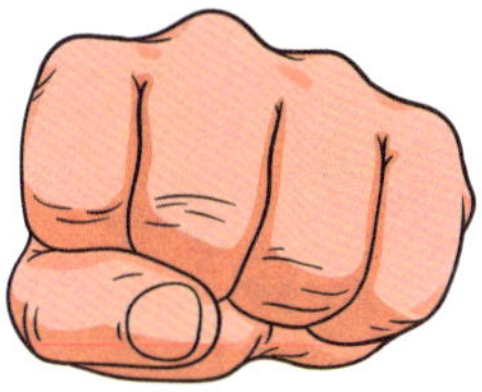

fist sing crib

1 crib

2 fist

3 sing

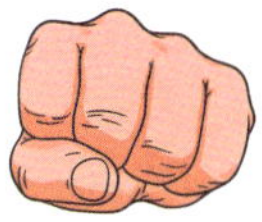

**Directions:** Circle the word for the picture. Write the word.

4

mist lift

 

**Directions:** Match the words to the pictures.

stop

chop

lock

1. stop

2. lock

3. chop

**Directions:** Circle the word for the picture. Write the word.

4. 

dock crop

____ ____ ____ ____

**Directions:** Trace each word. Then, write each word twice.



1. I
2. at
3. who
4. as
5. me

**Directions:** Write each lowercase letter.

1. B ______
2. E ______
3. G ______
4. H ______
5. I ______
6. R ______
7. T ______
8. Y ______

**Directions:** Trace the words about features of Earth.

mountain

lake

Earth

hill

glacier

**Directions:** Write about Earth. Fill in the checklist.

## Topic

Earth has ______________________ features.
(**a lot of** or **many**)

## Detail

Earth has ______________________
______________________________.

## Closing

Earth is ______________________.

### ☑ Checklist

- ☐ I have a topic sentence.
- ☐ I have a detail.
- ☐ I have a closing.

**Directions:** Solve each problem.

1. Circle the number that is one more than 4.

   3　　　4　　　5

2. Circle the number that comes after 6.

   3　　　5　　　7

3. I am the number that comes after 8. What number am I?

   ________

4. I am the number that comes after 5. What number am I?

   ________

5. John finds 4 seashells. Then, he finds one more. How many seashells does he have now?

   ________

6. Sandy started counting like this:

   1　　2　　3　　4　　5

   How is Sandy counting? Circle the answer.

   forward　　　backward

**Directions:** Solve each problem.

1. Circle the container that holds the most.

2. Circle the container that holds the most.

3. Circle the object that weighs the least.

4. Circle the shortest animal

5. Draw or write something that weighs less than a boy.

6. Draw a container that holds more than a bucket.

**Directions:** Look at the example. Solve the problem. Circle your answer.

**Example:** Count the berries. Start at 5. How many berries are there in all?

1 2 3 4 5 6 7 (8) 9 10

Count the crayons. Start at 3. How many crayons are there in all?

1 2 3 4 5 6 7 8 9 10

**Directions:** Draw a picture to show the problem. Circle your answer.

Draw 2 more bugs. Count the bugs. Start at 3. How many bugs are there in all?

3

Circle the answer.

1 2 3 4 5 6 7 8 9 10

**Directions:** Draw each natural feature.

| river | mountain |
| --- | --- |
| hill | lake |

**Directions:** Follow the steps in this experiment to discover how animals live.

## What You Need

an animal to observe
(such as a bird, an ant, or a lizard)

## What to Do

1. Find an animal to observe. Observe it for a few minutes.
2. Draw a picture of where the animal lives.
3. Tell about what the animal is doing.

**Directions:** Sort the letters. Put some in the first box. Put some in the second box. Tell a partner how you sorted the letters.

a c e h k m p s v z

| | |
|---|---|
| | |

**Directions:** Play with a partner. Do a scavenger hunt around the house. Look for the letters in the charts below. Each player should tally the letters he or she finds. The person with the most tallies at the end of five minutes wins.

**Player 1**

| | |
|---|---|
| B | |
| E | |
| G | |
| H | |
| M | |
| R | |
| T | |
| Y | |

**Player 2**

| | |
|---|---|
| B | |
| E | |
| G | |
| H | |
| M | |
| R | |
| T | |
| Y | |

 

## High-Frequency Words Activity

Have your child practice spelling the high-frequency words from page 69 in different silly voices.

## Writing Activity

Have your child review his or her writing from page 72. Have him or her circle the first letter of each sentence to make sure it begins with a capital letter.

## Mathematics Activity

Help your child gather two containers of different sizes. Help him or her find a way to prove that one container holds more than the other container.

## Problem-Solving Activity

Put some counters, such as buttons, beans, or O-shaped cereal into a container. Have your child grab a small handful and count the objects. Then, have him or her grab another handful and count on.

## Science Activity

Have your child observe a different animal. Ask your child to compare this animal to the one he or she observed in the experiment on page 78.

## Listening-and-Speaking Activity

Ask your child to name the natural features that you have in your local area or that you have visited. Ask your child how these features are different.

**Directions:** Read the text. Answer the questions on the next page.

# Gus and His Pets

Gus has two pets.

Gus can run and jump with one pet.

Ruff! Ruff!

One pet does not run or jump.

Quack! Quack!

**Directions:** Listen to and read "Gus and His Pets." Answer the questions.

1. Who has pets?
   - (A) a pup
   - (B) a duck
   - (C) Gus

2. What kinds of pets does Gus have?
   - (A) a pup and a duck
   - (B) a bug and a pup
   - (C) a duck and a cat

3. Which pet runs?
   - (A) a pup
   - (B) a duck
   - (C) a bug

4. Which is another good title?
   - (A) "Duck in the Pond"
   - (B) "Two Pets"
   - (C) "Gus Runs"

**Directions:** Trace each word. Read each sentence. Circle the word in each sentence.

1 from

It is from mom.

2 or

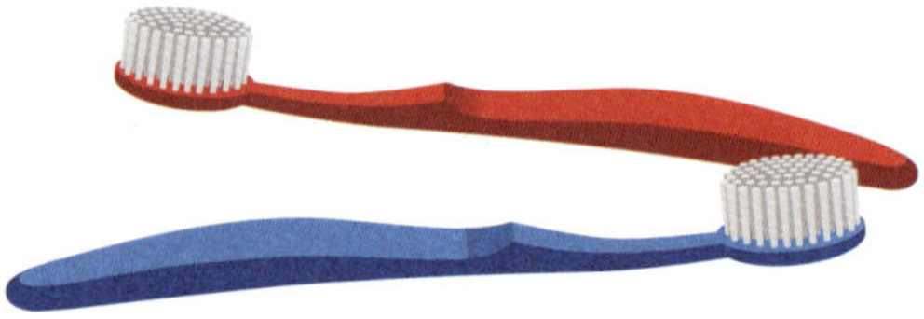

Do you like blue or red?

3 one

He has one truck.

4 had

I had a good day.

5 by

Sit by me.

 

**Directions:** Circle the noun in each sentence.

1. A boy digs.

2. The lamp is red.

3. A dog runs fast.

4. The girl plays with a toy.

5. The cat is slow.

6. The desk is full.

**Directions:** Circle the picture you like best. Write your opinion. Write a reason.

dog

cat

## Opinion

I like ____________________.

## Reason

I like it because ____________________

____________________.

**Directions:** Write about a dog or a cat. Fill in the checklist.

## Opinion

_____________________ is the best pet.
(**A dog** or **A cat**)

## Reason

I like it because _____________________
_____________________.

## Closing

I love _____________________.
(**dogs** or **cats**)

### ☑ Checklist

- ☐ I state my opinion.
- ☐ I have a reason.
- ☐ I have a closing.

**Directions:** Solve each problem by adding.

1 

________

3 + 2 = ________

4 

________

2 + 2 = ________

2 

________

1 + 3 = ________

5 

________

2 + 3 = ________

3 

________

4 + 1 = ________

6 

________

1 + 3 = ________

**Directions: Solve each problem.**

1. Does the solid have any flat surfaces? Circle the answer.

yes no

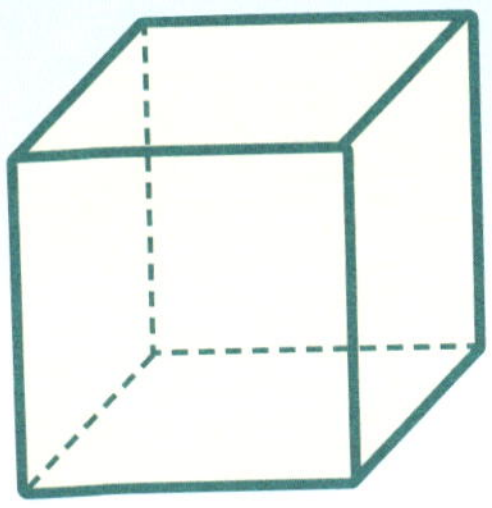

2. How many corners does a hexagon have?

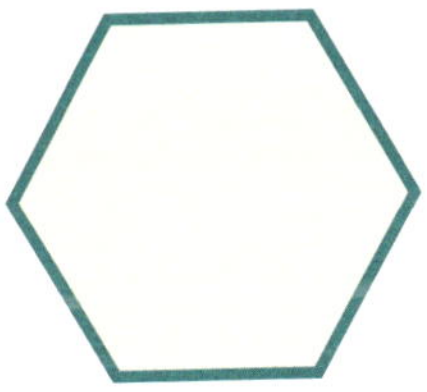

3. Circle the shape with 3 sides.

4. Does the solid have any curved surfaces? Circle the answer.

yes no

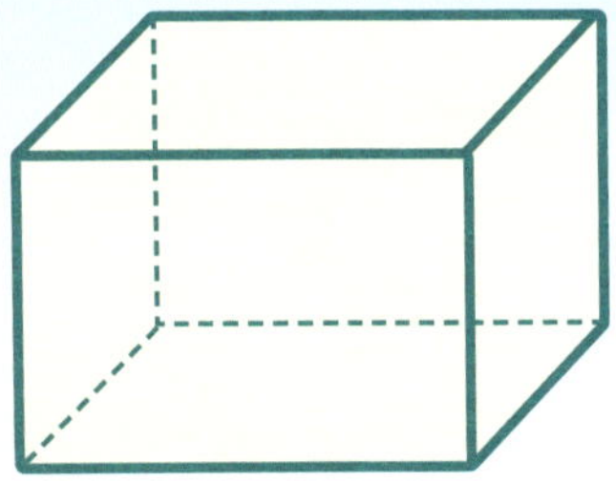

5. How many corners does a circle have?

6. Color the shapes with 4 sides.

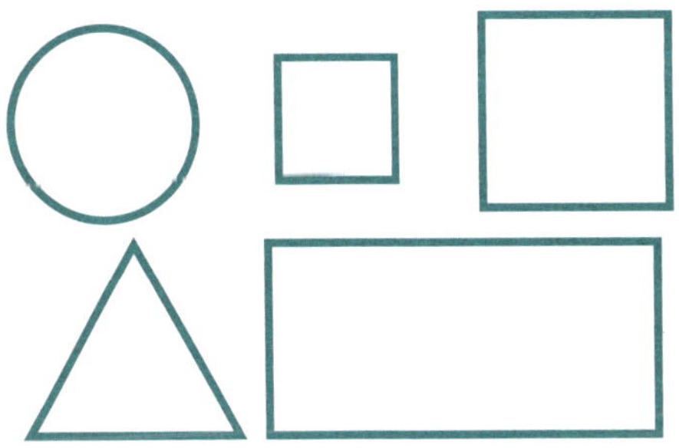

**Directions:** Read the problem. Solve the problem.

Jess has 3 cats. Bob has 1 cat. Leo has 4 cats. Who has the most cats? Who has the fewest cats?

Draw a picture to show the problem.

__________________ has the most cats.

__________________ has the fewest cats.

 

**Directions:** Read the problem. Solve the problem.

There are 4 slices of pizza in a box. Tom eats 2 slices. Maria eats 1 slice. How many slices of pizza are in the box now?

Draw a picture to show the problem.

________

________ slice of pizza

**Directions:** Draw lines to match the calendars to the correct words.

1

| January | | | | | | |
|---|---|---|---|---|---|---|
| S | M | T | W | Th | F | S |
| 1 | 2 | 3 | 4 | 5 | 6 | 7 |
| 8 | 9 | 10 | 11 | 12 | **13** | 14 |
| 15 | 16 | 17 | 18 | 19 | 20 | 21 |
| 22 | 23 | 24 | 25 | 26 | 27 | 28 |
| 29 | 30 | 31 | | | | |

month

2

| January | | | | | | |
|---|---|---|---|---|---|---|
| S | M | T | W | Th | F | S |
| 1 | 2 | 3 | 4 | 5 | 6 | 7 |
| **8** | **9** | **10** | **11** | **12** | **13** | **14** |
| 15 | 16 | 17 | 18 | 19 | 20 | 21 |
| 22 | 23 | 24 | 25 | 26 | 27 | 28 |
| 29 | 30 | 31 | | | | |

day

3

| January | | | | | | |
|---|---|---|---|---|---|---|
| S | M | T | W | Th | F | S |
| **1** | **2** | **3** | **4** | **5** | **6** | **7** |
| **8** | **9** | **10** | **11** | **12** | **13** | **14** |
| **15** | **16** | **17** | **18** | **19** | **20** | **21** |
| **22** | **23** | **24** | **25** | **26** | **27** | **28** |
| **29** | **30** | **31** | | | | |

week

**Directions:** Draw a picture for each of the following.

| Draw something you do every day. | Draw something you do every week. | Draw one thing you will do this month. |
|---|---|---|
| | | |

**Directions:** Follow the steps in this experiment to discover how the weather changes.

## What to Do

1. Look outside each day.
2. Choose a symbol for each kind of weather. Use your symbols to draw the weather in the chart each day.

| Monday | Tuesday | Wednesday | Thursday | Friday |
|---|---|---|---|---|
| | | | | |

3. How did the weather change this week?

**Directions:** Each row must have each shape ♡ ☺. Each column much have each shape ♡ ☺.

**Directions:** Play with a partner. Put a paper clip on the X. Put a pencil through the paper clip to make a spinner. Put 20 small objects into a bag. Each player reaches into the bag and pulls out some objects. Then, spin the spinner. If your objects match the spin, you get a point. Put the objects back, and start again. Take turns until someone gets 10 points.

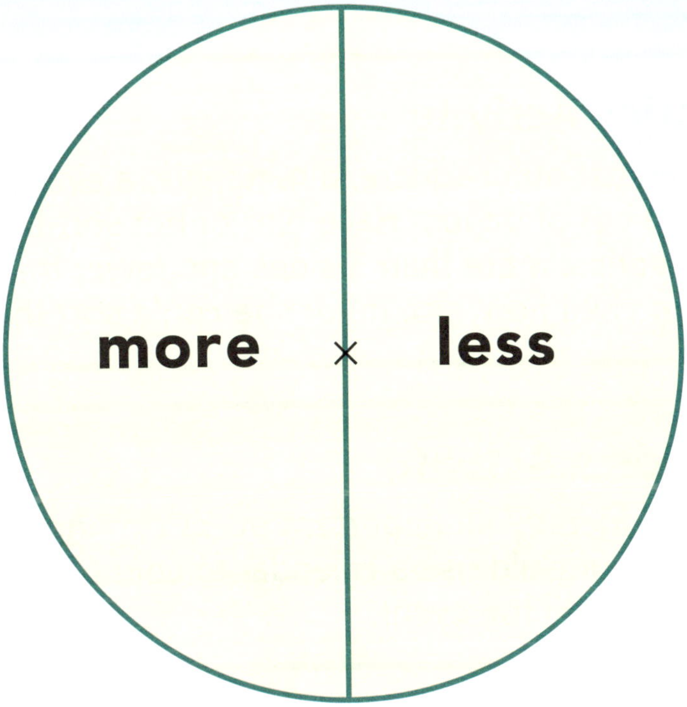


| Points | |
|---|---|
| **Player 1:** | **Player 2:** |
| | |

## High-Frequency Words Activity

Review the high-frequency words on page 84 with your child. Have him or her write the words with sidewalk chalk on the sidewalk or driveway.

## Writing Activity

Help your child review his or her writing from page 87. Have him or her circle the nouns in each sentence.

## Mathematics Activity

Help your child cut out a square, a rectangle, a circle, a triangle, and a hexagon out of paper. Have him or her sort the shapes into two categories: more than 3 sides and fewer than 3 sides. Then, ask your child how else he or she could sort the shapes.

## Social Studies Activity

Help your child identify an important event coming up, such as a holiday. Have your child use a calendar to count the number of days and weeks until the event.

## Science Activity

Have your child track the weather during a different week. If possible, choose a week with much different weather. Ask your child how the weather is different from the first week he or she observed.

## Listening-and-Speaking Activity

Ask your child why he or she prefers dogs or cats. Ask your child what he or she would say to convince a person who disagreed with his or her opinion.

 

**Directions:** Read the text. Answer the questions on the next page.



## A Hen

This is a hen.

The baby is a chick.

They live in a pen.

They peck for seeds and corn.

**Directions:** Listen to and read "A Hen." Answer the questions.

1. What is the baby called?
   - Ⓐ a hen
   - Ⓑ a kid
   - Ⓒ a chick

2. Where do the hens live?
   - Ⓐ in a box
   - Ⓑ in the dirt
   - Ⓒ in a pen

3. How do hens get seeds and corn?
   - Ⓐ They dig.
   - Ⓑ They peck.
   - Ⓒ They hunt.

4. What is this text about?
   - Ⓐ pens
   - Ⓑ hens
   - Ⓒ seeds and corn

**Directions:** Look at the shape of the word. Find the box with that shape. Write each letter in a box.

| not | but | what | we |
|---|---|---|---|

**Example:** w o r d

1

2

3

4

UNIT 7

Language

**Directions:** Add punctuation.

1. I like the pink cap
2. Who will win
3. The tent is wet
4. Do not yell
5. Who can mop
6. Why did you go
7. I love to read
8. The pen is blue

**Directions:** Think about a time you went to a birthday party. Draw notes about the day.

## Who?

## Where?

## When?

## Event 1

## Event 2

**Directions:** Write about a birthday party. Fill in the checklist.

## Introduction

I went to a birthday party for

______________________________________________.

## Events

______________________________________________

First, __________________________________________.

Then, __________________________________________.

## Closing Sentence

______________________________________________

had a great birthday!

### Checklist

- [ ] I have an introduction.
- [ ] I have events.
- [ ] I have a closing.

**Directions:** Solve each problem.

1. How many rings are there?

14 15 16

2. How many snails are there?

17 18 19

3. How many bugs are there?

18 19 20

4. Color 10 balls.

5. Circle 14 bees.

6. Circle 13 sea stars.

**Directions:** Solve each problem by subtracting.

1 

$3 - 2 =$ ______

4 

$3 - 0 =$ ______

2 

$5 - 3 =$ ______

5 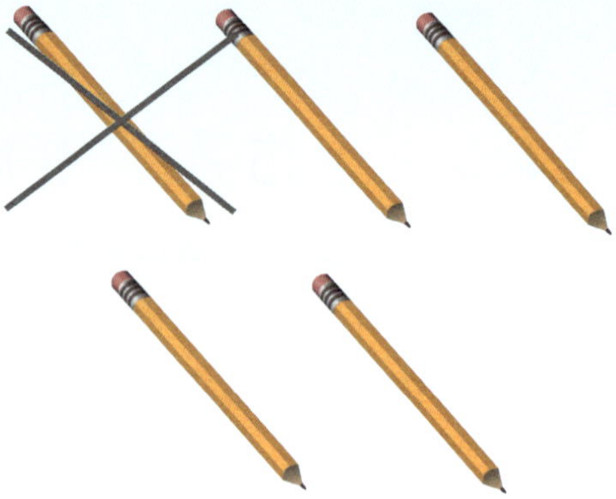

$5 - 1 =$ ______

3 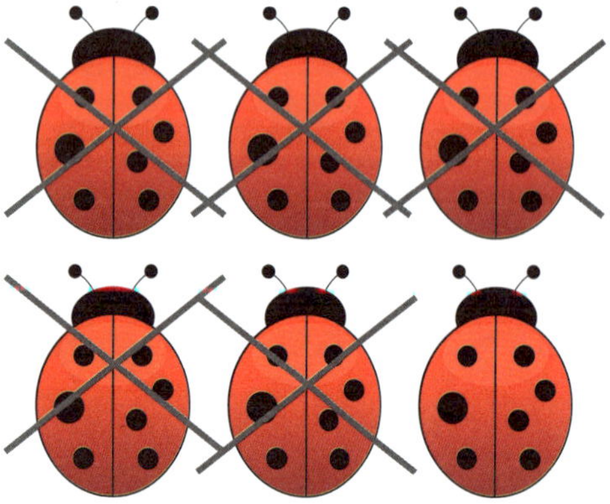

$6 - 5 =$ ______

6 

$5 - 5 =$ ______

**Directions:** Read the problem. Solve the problem.

There are 8 frogs on a log. Two frogs are green. One frog is orange. The rest of the frogs are red. How many frogs are red?

Draw a picture to show the problem.

2 + 1 + ________ = 8

There are ____________ red frogs.

**Directions:** Read the problem. Solve the problem.

Kai wants to sort leaves by size.

1. How many groups should Kai make?

______

2. Sort the leaves into groups.

3. Which group has the fewest leaves? Circle the group.

4. Which group has the most leaves? Write an X on the group.

 

**Directions:** Write the names of the American symbols. Color the symbols.

## American Symbols

- bald eagle
- American flag
- Statue of Liberty
- Liberty Bell

1 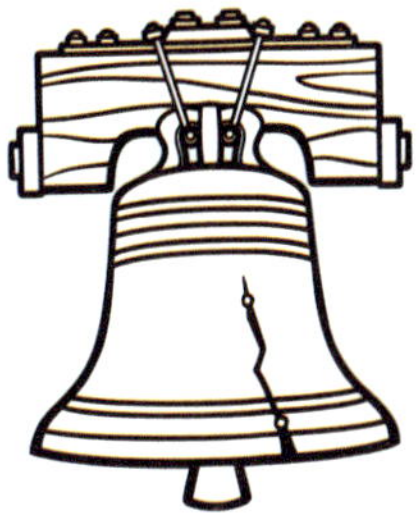

2 

3 

4 

UNIT 7

Science

**Directions:** Follow the steps in this experiment to see how objects roll.

## What You Need

- objects
- board
- newspaper
- paint

## What to Do

1. Angle the board with some books or a rock. You have made a ramp.
2. Cover the ramp with newspaper. Place newspaper around the ramp, especially at the bottom.
3. Paint one side of an object. Let it go down the ramp.
4. Repeat step #3 with two more objects. Use different colors of paint on each one. Watch them go down the ramp.
5. Draw how they went down the ramp.

**Directions:** Write the name of each baby animal. Use word clues to help you.

## Baby Animals

- piglet
- owlet
- chick
- spiderling
- joey
- pup

1 

2 

3 

4 

5 

6 

**Directions:** Play with a partner. Place a paper clip on the X. Place a pencil through the paper clip to make a spinner. Take turns spinning the spinner. Read the word it lands on. Place a check mark next to the word in your chart. The first player to get two check marks next to each word wins.

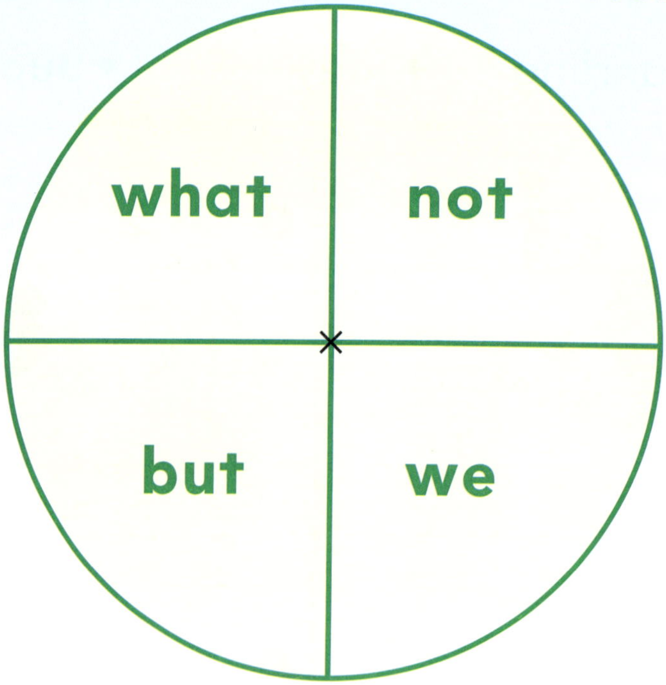


| Player 1 | |
|---|---|
| | |
| what | |
| not | |
| but | |
| we | |

| Player 1 | |
|---|---|
| | |
| what | |
| not | |
| but | |
| we | |

 

## High-Frequency Words Activity

Use your finger to write the high-frequency words from page 99 on your child's back. Have your child guess the words you write. Then, have your child write words on your back.

## Writing Activity

Help your child review his or her writing from page 102. Have him or her circle the punctuation after each sentence.

## Mathematics Activity

Help your child write a subtraction problem by drawing pictures and then crossing some off. Have your child write an equation to match the picture.

## Problem-Solving Activity

Help your child collect objects from around the house. Have him or her sort the objects in some way. Ask your child how each group is sorted. Then, have him or her count the number of objects in each group.

## Social Studies Activity

Go on a scavenger hunt as you drive around the community this week. Ask your child to locate as many symbols that represent your country as he or she can.

## Listening-and-Speaking Activity

Ask your child to describe his or her dream birthday party. What would he or she do? Who would be there? What gifts would your child get?

**Directions:** Read the text. Answer the questions on the next page.

## Pib Likes to Dig

Pib likes to dig.

He digs in the bin.

Get him out of the bin!

Kim puts Pib in the sink.

Meow!

 

**Directions:** Listen to and read "Pib Likes to Dig." Answer the questions.



1. Who likes to dig?
   - (A) Pib
   - (B) Kim
   - (C) the bin

2. Where does Pib dig?
   - (A) in the sink
   - (B) in the bin
   - (C) with Kim

3. Why does Kim put Pib in the sink?
   - (A) Pib got dirty.
   - (B) Pib likes the sink.
   - (C) Pib wants to dig.

4. Which is another good title?
   - (A) "Cat"
   - (B) "Messy Pib"
   - (C) "Kim's Job"

**Directions:** Trace each word. Write each word. Then, write a sentence using one of the words.

1. all
2. were
3. can
4. your
5. when

**Directions:** Write the verb.

1 The bug ______________________.

(**rug** or **ran**)

2 The baby ______________________.

(**dad** or **naps**)

3 Mom will ______________________ it.

(**cat** or **fix**)

4 The man ______________________ me.

(**helps** or **hand**)

5 Tim ______________________ the pen.

(**gum** or **grabs**)

**Directions:** Trace the words about ducks.

rock

pond

bread

feather

**Directions:** Write about ducks. Fill in the checklist.

## Topic

Ducks are ______________________________.

## Detail

They ______________________________

______________________________.

## Closing

I love ______________________________.

### Checklist

- [ ] I have a topic sentence.
- [ ] I have a detail.
- [ ] I have a closing.

**Directions:** Solve each problem.

1. Count the donuts. Draw an equal set of circles.

3. Count the balloons. Draw a set of circles that is more than the balloons.

2. Draw a set of 2 triangles. Draw a set of more than 2 circles.

| **2** |
| --- |
| |
| **More than 2** |
| |

4. Color an equal number of circles.

**Directions:** Solve each problem.

1

____ + ____ = ____

2

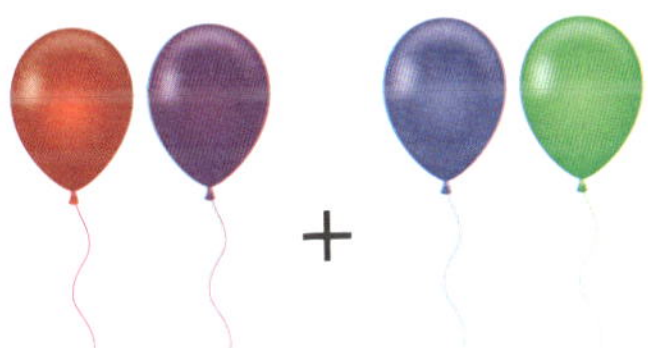

____ + ____ = ____

3 Circle the number sentence that matches the picture.

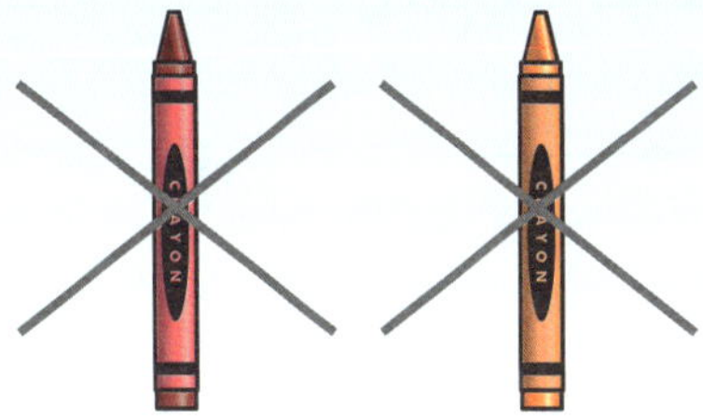

2 + 2 = 4

2 – 0 = 2

2 – 2 = 0

4 Draw a picture to show 1 + 1 = 2

**Directions:** Read the problem. Solve the problem.

There are 10 beads in a bag. Deanne has 90 beads in all. How many bags does she have?

Draw a picture to show the problem.

__________

__________ bags

 

**Directions:** Read the problem. Solve the problem.

1. Draw an object that is long and light.

2. Draw an object that is short and heavy.

3. Draw an object that is long and heavy.

4. Draw an object that is short and light.

**Directions:** Color the things that are *needs*. Circle the things that are *wants*.

**Directions:** Follow the steps in this experiment to discover how you can group rocks.

## What You Need

- lots of rocks
- magnifying glass
- water
- shallow bowl

## What to Do

1. Look at the rocks. Use a magnifying glass to look closely.

2. Put the rocks into three groups: small, bigger, and biggest. Draw them in the boxes.

| Small Rocks | Bigger Rocks | Biggest Rocks |
|---|---|---|
| | | |

3. Put the rocks into a bowl. Pour some water on them.

4. Put the wet rocks into groups of different colors. Tell a family member about the groups you made.

**Directions:** Think about each object in the box. Write the objects in the orders listed.

| ruler | ant | door | mug |
|---|---|---|---|

1. Shortest to Tallest

2. Lightest to Heaviest

**Directions:** Play with a partner. Take turns rolling two number cubes. Add the dots on both cubes. Cross off the sum in your box. The first player to cross off all the numbers wins. Play two times.

**Player 1:** ____________________

7 8 9 10 11 12

**Player 2:** ____________________

7 8 9 10 11 12

**Player 1:** ____________________

7 8 9 10 11 12

**Player 2:** ____________________

7 8 9 10 11 12

## High-Frequency Words Activity

Have your child use cereal pieces to form the letters of each high-frequency word from page 114. Have him or her practice reading the words. Then, he or she can eat the words!

## Writing Activity

Help your child review his or her writing from page 117. Ask your child to identify the verbs he or she wrote. Have your child act out each verb.

## Problem-Solving Activity

Talk to your child about comparisons. Have your child name objects that are taller, shorter, lighter, and heavier than himself or herself.

## Social Studies Activity

Ask your child to think about the things he or she uses every day. Ask your child which are needs and which are wants.

## Critical-Thinking Activity

Review the activity on page 124 with your child. Choose three new objects, and have your child repeat the activity. Discuss why the lists for tallest and heaviest may differ.

## Listening-and-Speaking Activity

Ask your child to explain how he or she sorted the rocks in the science experiment on page 123.

 

**Directions:** Read the text. Answer the questions on the next page.

Reading

# The Ox

An ox can pull a rock.

It can pull a log.

It can help with a crop.

An ox is strong!

**Directions:** Listen to and read "The Ox." Answer the questions.

1. What animal is this story about?
   - (A) an ox
   - (B) a log
   - (C) a cat

2. What can an ox pull?
   - (A) a crop
   - (B) a rock
   - (C) a baby

3. Who does the ox help?
   - (A) the rock
   - (B) a farmer
   - (C) another ox

4. Which is another good title?
   - (A) "Strong Ox"
   - (B) "Move Rocks"
   - (C) "Animals"

**Directions:** Read the words in the box. Find the hidden words. Circle the hidden words.

| use | said | there | an | each |
|---|---|---|---|---|

1. t u d k e h k a n w t d e t h
2. s r i u s e q u j e z h p e i b
3. w e n b u x v d e a c h i n z
4. a i n b n s a i d k m i p u r w
5. d k i p q u g t h e r e i e o h a

UNIT 9

Language

**Directions:** Circle the words that are spelled correctly.

1. rak
   rake

2. rat
   ratt

3. tope
   top

4. het
   hit

5. bike
   bice

**Directions:** Circle the picture you like best. Write your opinion. Write a reason.

ice cream

a cookie

## Opinion

I like ______________________.

## Reason

I like it because ______________________

______________________

______________________.

**Directions:** Write about ice cream or cookies. Fill in the checklist.

## Opinion

_______________________ is the best.
(**Ice cream** or **A cookie**)

## Reason

I like it because _______________________
_______________________.

## Closing

I love _______________________
_______________________.

## ☑ Checklist

- ☐ I state my opinion.
- ☐ I have a reason.
- ☐ I have a closing.

**Directions:** Solve each problem.

1. How many sunflowers are there?

2. How many lizards are there?

3. Count how many.

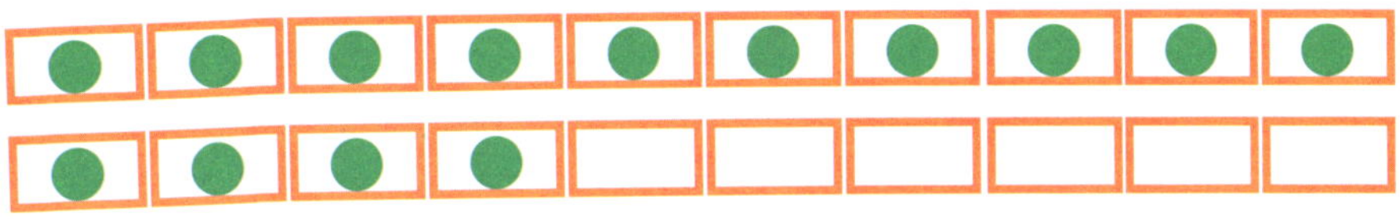

4. How many snails are there?

5. Count how many.

6. Count how many.

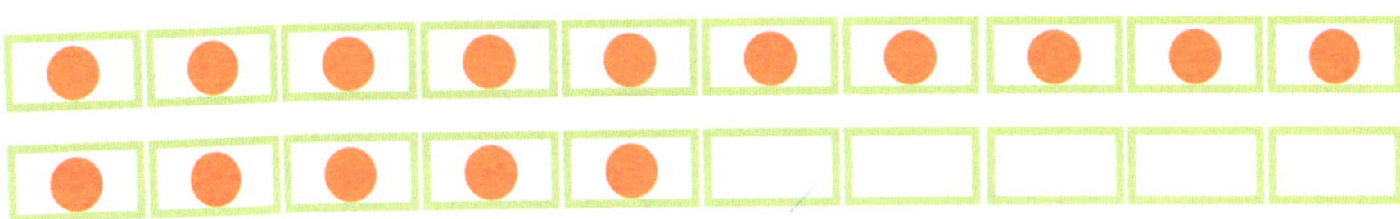

**Directions:** Solve each problem.

1. How many fish are left?

2. How many crayons are left?

3. Circle the number sentence that matches the picture.

2 – 1 = 1

2 + 1 = 3

3 – 1 = 2

4. Circle the number sentence that matches the picture.

3 + 0 = 3

3 – 3 = 0

3 – 0 = 3

5. Draw a picture to show 5 – 1 = 4.

6. Draw a picture to show 4 – 2 = 2.

**Directions:** Read the problem. Solve the problem.

Kiki has 4 dresses. Two are green, and the rest are red. How many red dresses does Kiki have?

Draw a picture to show the problem.

Kiki has __________ red dresses.

**Directions:** Read the problem. Solve the problem.

Mita has 9 balloons. Three are red. Three are yellow. The rest are blue. How many are blue?

Draw a picture to show the problem.

______

_ _ _ _ _

There are ______ blue balloons.

**Directions:** Draw the job each community helper does.

1 

doctor

2 

firefighter

3 

mail carrier

4 

police officer

**Directions:** Follow this experiment to see what a person needs.

## What to Do

1. Observe yourself for a day. Draw pictures of what you need to survive.

| air | shelter |
| --- | --- |
| food | water |

2. Could you live without all of the things listed above? Why or why not?

 

**Directions:** The same letter is missing in each set of words. Write it on the lines to complete the words.

**1**

____ at

____ ap

____ amp

**2**

m ____ p

st ____ p

n ____ d

**3**

s ____ t

b ____ t

l ____ p

**Directions:** Play with a partner. Put a paper clip on each X. Put a pencil through each paper clip to make a spinner. Flick each spinner in order. Write the word you spun on a sheet of paper. Take turns making as many words as you can in two minutes. Circle the real words. The person with the most real words wins.

1

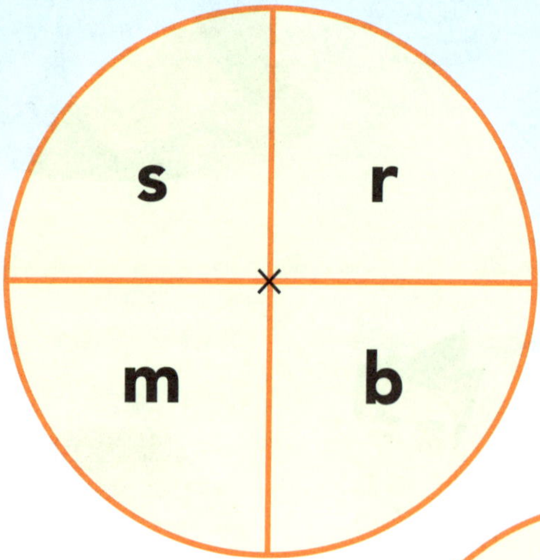


2

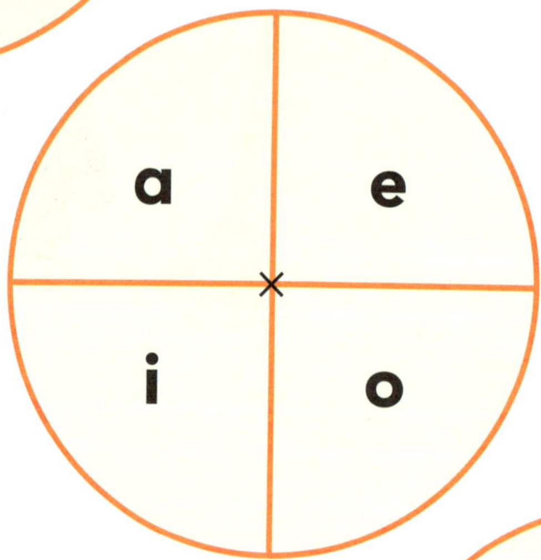


3

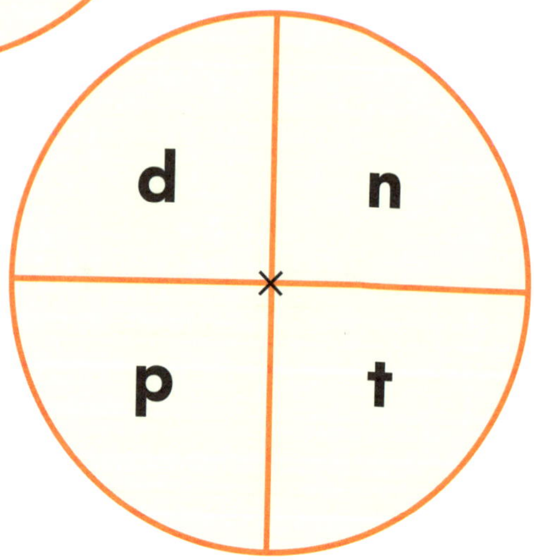

## High-Frequency Words Activity

Review the high-frequency words from page 129 with your child. Have him or her write the words using a variety of writing tools, such as a pen, a pencil, paint, a marker, and crayons.

## Writing Activity

Revisit page 132. Work with your child to spell as many words as possible correctly. Focus on sight words or spelling rules that your child knows.

## Mathematics Activity

Tell your child the ages of three friends or family members. Ask your child whether each age is greater than, less than, or equal to his or her age.

## Social Studies Activity

Ask your child to name two other community helpers and discuss the jobs they each do.

## Critical-Thinking Activity

Ask your child to brainstorm more words that share one letter. Challenge him or her to think of as many as possible.

## Listening-and-Speaking Activity

Ask your child what community helper job he or she would most like to have and why.

**Directions:** Read the text. Answer the questions on the next page.

# Camping

Sam and Pam love to camp at the beach.

They swim.

Dad makes a campfire.

They fix hot dogs.

Yum!

 

**Directions:** Listen to and read "Camping." Answer the questions.

1 Who makes the campfire?

(A) Sam

(B) Pam

(C) Dad

2 Where do they camp?

(A) at the beach

(B) at the forest

(C) in the yard

3 How do the hot dogs taste?

(A) bad

(B) okay

(C) very good

4 What is this story about?

(A) swimming

(B) camping at the beach

(C) making hot dogs

**Directions:** Read the sentences. Circle the high-frequency words in each sentence. Write each word two times.

| which | she | do | how | their |
|---|---|---|---|---|

1. How can we fix this?

2. She is my friend.

3. Their play was good.

4. Which one is bigger?

5. Can you do it?

 

**Directions:** Write the plural noun.

1. You have two ____________________.
(**dime** or **dimes**)

2. The ____________________ are red.
(**ant** or **ants**)

3. He has three ice cream ____________________.
(**cones** or **cone**)

4. Let's play two ____________________.
(**game** or **games**)

5. I see five ____________________.
(**lakes** or **lake**)

**Directions:** Trace the words about washing your hands.

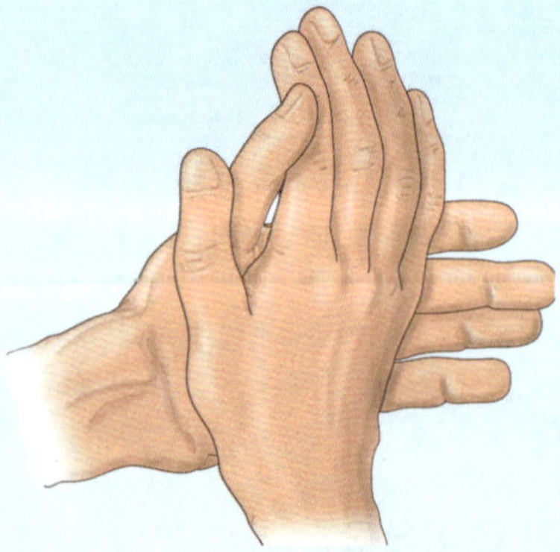

hands

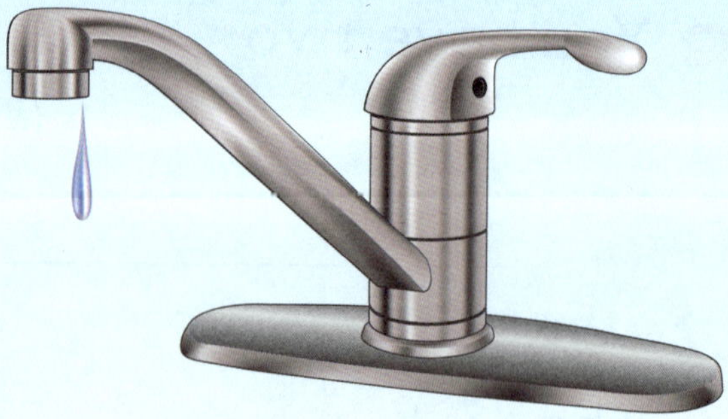

water

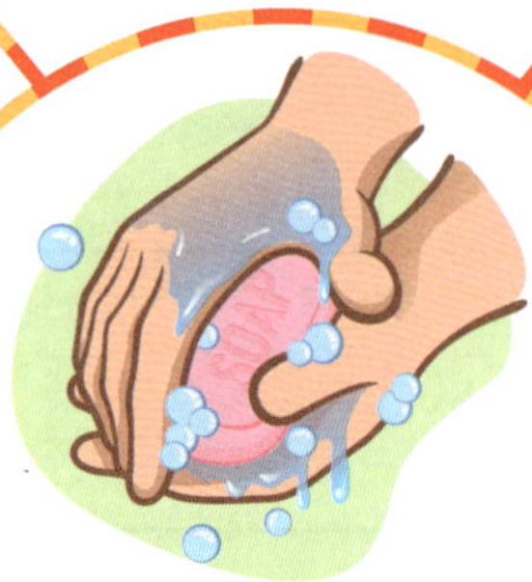

washing your hands

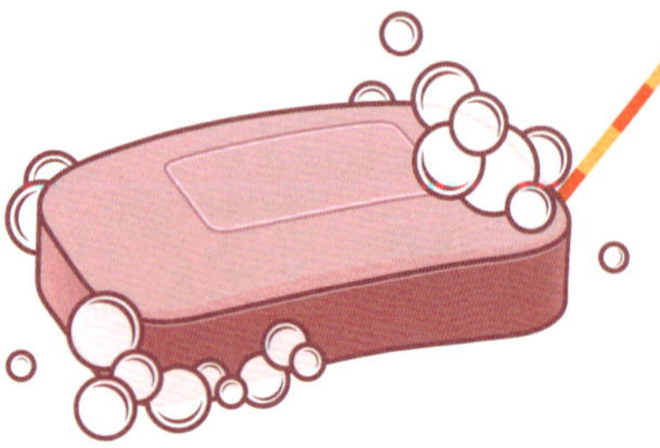

soap

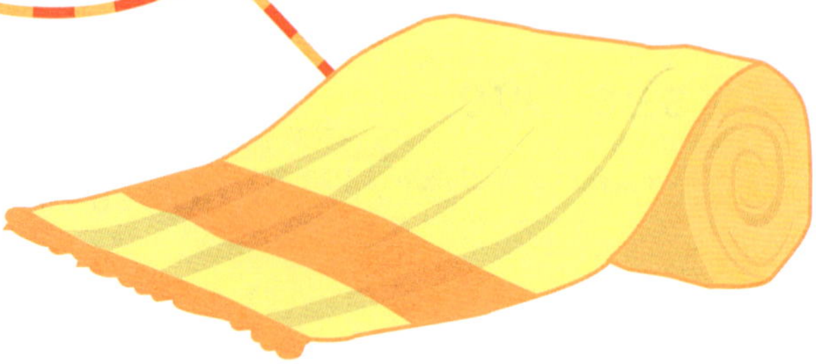

towel

**Directions:** Write about washing your hands. Fill in the checklist.

## Topic

Washing your hands is ______________________.

## Detail

You must ______________________

______________________.

## Closing

Make sure you ______________________.

### Checklist

- [ ] I have a topic sentence.
- [ ] I have a detail.
- [ ] I have a closing.

**Directions:** Solve each problem.

1. Circle the larger number.

   5 9

2. Circle the smaller number.

   10 8

3. Circle the smaller number.

   7 6

4. Circle the larger number.

   11 9

5. Circle the smallest number.

   5 8 12

6. Circle the largest number.

   6 12 16

**Directions:** Solve each problem.

1. Marcy drinks 3 glasses of water. Later, she drinks 2 more glasses of water. How many glasses of water did Marcy drink?

3. Kiko had 3 jackets. She lost one. How many jackets does she still have?

2. A pizza was cut into 6 pieces. Michelle ate 2 of the pieces. How many pieces are left?

4. Draw a picture to match. There are 3 fish swimming. Then, 2 more fish come.

**Directions:** Read the problem. Solve the problem. Circle your answer.

Ray puts 18 pancakes on 3 plates. The first plate has 10 pancakes. The next plate has 3 pancakes. How many pancakes are on the last plate?

1. Draw a picture to show the problem.

2. Write a number sentence to solve the problem.

10 + ____ + ____ = 18

3. Write your answer.

There are ____ pancakes on the last plate.

 

**Directions:** Read the problem. Solve the problem.

What shapes can you make with triangles?

1. Draw a shape using triangles.

2. Draw another shape using triangles.

3. Draw a third shape using triangles.

**Directions:** Color the things you have in your community.

**Directions:** Follow the steps in this experiment to discover how to tell where things are.

## What You Need

- items of different sizes or colors
- crayons or markers

## What to Do

1. Work with a partner. Brainstorm words that can tell about where things are. Write the words.

2. Take turns placing an object on a table. Say facts about its location. Repeat for each object.

3. Draw a picture to show where all the objects are.

UNIT 10

Critical Thinking

**Directions:** Write the numbers 1–9 each on a slip of paper. Follow the directions below.

1. Mix up the numbers. Then, write them in order counting forward.

2. Mix up the numbers. Then, write them in order counting backward.

3. Put the numbers back in the jar. Take out 2 numbers. Write the largest two-digit number you can make.

4. Write the smallest two-digit number you can make.

**Directions:** Set up 10 water bottles like bowling pins. Take turns rolling a ball toward the bottles. Count how many are left standing. Write an X on that number on your scorecard. Reset the pins after each turn. The first player to mark off all the numbers wins.

**Player 1:** ____________________

0 1 2 3 4 5 6 7 8 9 10

**Player 2:** ____________________

0 1 2 3 4 5 6 7 8 9 10

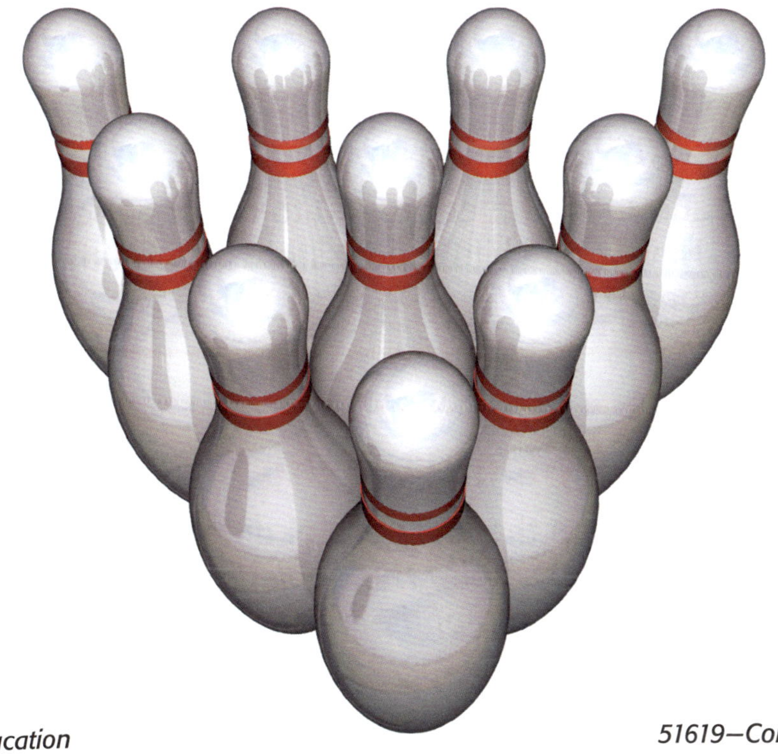

## High-Frequency Words Activity

Read a book aloud to your child. Have him or her find any high-frequency words from page 144 in the book.

## Writing Activity

Help your child revisit his or her writing from page 147. Have your child circle any high-frequency words that he or she used. If your child did not use any, help him or her add a sentence or revise one to include one of the words.

## Problem-Solving Activity

Have your child draw pictures using squares. Then, have your child draw pictures using circles. Challenge your child to draw a picture using triangles, squares, and circles.

## Social Studies Activity

Ask your child to name other places or landmarks in your community. Talk about what makes your community unique.

## Critical-Thinking Activity

Have your child add the numbers 10–20 to his or her collection from page 154. Have your child repeat steps 1–4 on the page, using all 20 numbers.

## Listening-and-Speaking Activity

Ask your child to compare the locations of different objects around your home. For example, *The apple is closer to me than the butter* or *The cup is on top of the table.*

 

# Answer Key



There are many open-ended pages, problems, and writing prompts in this book. For those activities, the answers will vary. Answers are only given in this answer key if they are specific.

**page 7**

1. top
2. mop
3. pop
4. hop

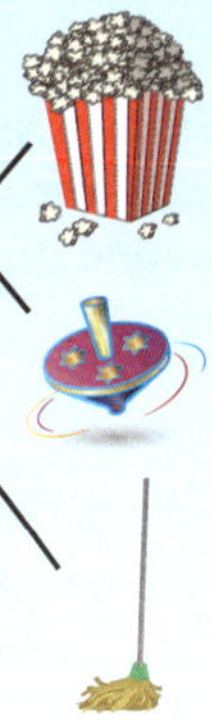

**page 8**

1. big
2. bib
3. bit
4. bin

**page 9**

| | |
|---|---|
| the | of |
| of | the |
| and | and |
| a | to |
| to | a |

**page 10**

1. in
2. by
3. on
4. under
5. behind

**page 13**

1. 3
2. 4
3. 5
4. 3
5. 5
6. 2

**page 14**

1. yes
2. no
3. no
4. yes

**page 15**

Picture should show seven bears, each wearing a hat.
There are 7 hats.

**page 16**

9; Student should have circled 9 flowers and drawn one leaf on each flower.

**page 19**

1. May
2. Madison
3. Morgan
4. Mary

**page 22**

1. pop
2. jog
3. Mom
4. log

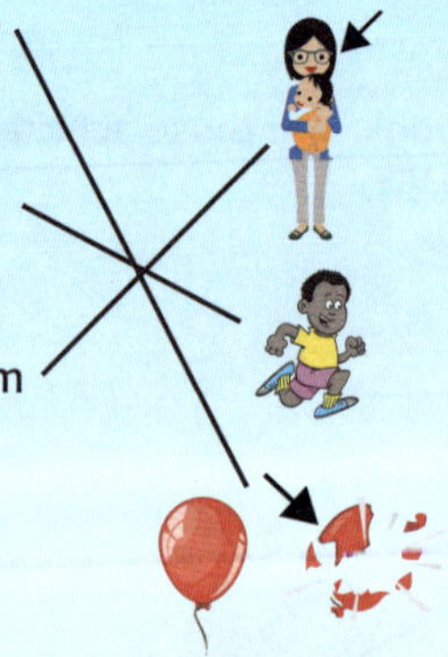

**page 23**

1. ten
2. vet
3. Ken
4. bed

**page 25**

1. The
2. A
3. We
4. Can
5. I

**page 26**

All words except *lollipop* should be traced.

**page 28**

1. One string should be drawn on the kite.
2. Two legs should be drawn on the person.
3. All three blocks should be colored.
4. Four apples should be colored.
5. One more circle should be drawn for a total of five.
6. Six legs should be drawn on the ladybug.

**page 29**

1. pentagons
2. rectangles
3. circles
4. squares
5. Students should draw an oval on the left and a rectangle on the right.

**page 30**

5 is greater than 4; Student should have drawn lines to match each fish to a corresponding crab and drawn a circle around the group of fish to show the group is greater.

**page 31**

Rick; Two apples should be drawn for Ken and four apples should be drawn for Rick.

**page 32**

1. 
2. 
3. 
4. 

**page 34**

1. There should be an X over the circle.
2. There should be an X over the triangle.
3. There should be an X over the pentagon.
4. There should be an X over the pentagon.

**page 37**

1. hut
2. mug
3. tug
4. cup

**page 38**

1. top
2. tap
3. tip
4. tag

**page 39**

1. this
2. he
3. was
4. for
5. on

**page 43**

1. 10
2. 15
3. 12
4. 17
5. 14
6. 19

**page 44**

1. 8
2. 8
3. 9
4. 7
5. 9
6. 6

**page 45**

Eight flowers should be drawn.
Kenny has 8 flowers now.

**page 46**

5; Student should have drawn 5 blocks and counted them.

**page 52**

1. bat
2. bet
3. bit
4. bug

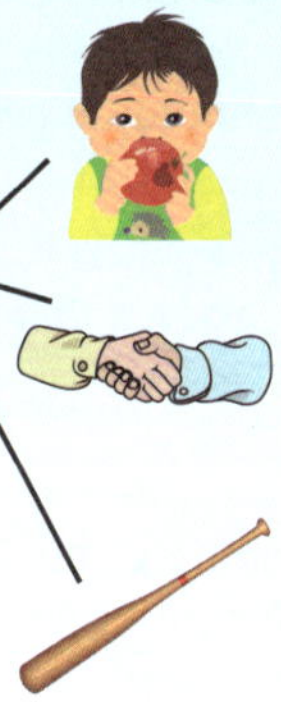

**page 53**

1. cot
2. cut
3. cat
4. can

**page 54**

1. lratiaremesa
2. hwithwtsklmt
3. yecslhyathey
4. pmrsihavenpa
5. rsahwhishses

**page 55**

1. up
2. hot
3. big
4. go
5. top

**page 58**

1. The group on the left should be circled.
2. The box on the right should be circled.
3. There should be an X on the group on the left.
4. The bowl on the right should be circled.

**page 59**

1. 9
2. The machine on the left should be circled.
3. 20
4. All the fish should be circled.

**page 60**

A cube has 6 faces. A sphere has 0 faces. The cube should be circled.

**page 61**

1. 0 corners; nothing should be circled
2. 8 corners; 8 corners should be circled
3. 0 corners; nothing should be circled

**page 64**

| Shape | Will it stack? | Will it slide? | Will it roll? |
|---|---|---|---|
| 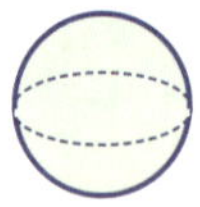 | No | No | Yes |
| 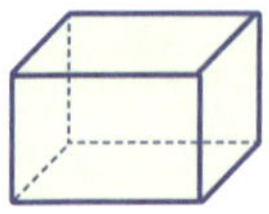 | Yes | Yes | No |
| 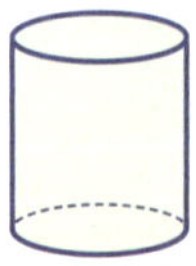 | Yes | Yes | Yes |
| 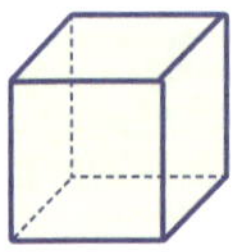 | Yes | Yes | No |

**page 67**

1. crib
2. fist
3. sing
4. lift

**page 68**

1. stop
2. lock
3. chop
4. crop

**page 69**

Student should have traced each word and written it twice on the lines.

**page 70**

1. b
2. e
3. g
4. h
5. i
6. r
7. t
8. y

**page 71**

All words should be traced.

**page 73**

1. 5
2. 7
3. 9
4. 6
5. 5
6. forward

**page 74**

1. The bathtub should be circled.
2. The milk carton should be circled.
3. The paper clip should be circled.
4. The mouse should be circled.
5. Example: a hat
6. Example: a swimming pool

**page 75**

7; Student should have counted on from 3.

**Page 76**

5; Student should have drawn 2 more bugs and counted on from 3.

**page 83**

1. C
2. A
3. A
4. B

**page 84**

1. It is from mom.
2. Do you like blue or red?
3. He has one truck.
4. I had a good day.
5. Sit by me.

**page 85**

1. boy
2. lamp
3. dog
4. girl
5. cat
6. desk

**page 88**

1. 5
2. 4
3. 5
4. 4
5. 5
6. 4

**page 89**

1. yes
2. 6
3. The triangle should be circled.
4. no
5. 0
6. Both squares and the rectangle should be colored.

**page 90**

Picture should show that Jess has 3 cats, Bob has 1 cat, and Leo has 4 cats.
Leo has the most cats.
Bob has the fewest cats.

**page 91**

Picture should show 4 slices of pizza. Three should be crossed out.
1 slice of pizza

**page 92**

1. day
2. week
3. month

**page 94**

**page 98**

1. C
2. C
3. B
4. B

**page 99**

1. we
2. but
3. what
4. not

**page 100**

1. I like the pink cap.
2. Who will win?
3. The tent is wet.
4. Do not yell!
5. Who can mop?
6. Why did you go?
7. I love to read!
8. The pen is blue.

**page 103**

1. 15
2. 17
3. 18
4. All but three balls should be colored.
5. 14 bees (all but one) should be circled.
6. 13 sea stars (all but three) should be circled.

**page 104**

1. 1
2. 2
3. 1
4. 3
5. 4
6. 0

**page 105**

Student should have drawn 2 green frogs, 1 orange frog, and 5 red frogs for a total of 8 frogs.
2 + 1 + 5 = 8
There are 5 red frogs.

**page 106**

1. 4
2. There should be 4 groups: 4 tiny leaves in one group, 2 small leaves in a second group, 3 medium leaves in a third group, and 1 large leaf in the fourth group.
3. There should be a circle around the group with 1 large leaf.
4. There should be an *X* on the group with 4 tiny leaves.

**page 107**

1. Liberty Bell
2. American Flag
3. Statue of Liberty
4. bald eagle

**page 109**

1. chick
2. owlet
3. joey
4. pup
5. spiderling
6. piglet

**page 113**

1. A
2. B
3. A
4. B

**page 115**

1. ran
2. naps
3. fix
4. helps
5. grabs

**page 116**

All words should be traced.

**page 118**

1. Six circles should be drawn.
2. Two triangles should be drawn on the left, and more than two circles should be drawn on the right.
3. A set of circles that is more than 7 should be drawn.
4. 15 circles should be colored.

**page 119**

1. 4 + 1 = 5
2. 2 + 2 = 4
3. 2 − 2 = 0
4. Student should have drawn two sets of one object each for a total of two objects.

**page 120**

Student should have drawn groups of 10 beads in 9 bags for a total of 90 beads.
9 bags

**page 121**

1. Possible answer: pencil; feather; stick
2. Possible answer: rock, big book, brick
3. Possible answer: airplane, truck; boat
4. Possible answer: seashell, penny; eraser

**page 122**

Clothes, water bottle, house, shoes and food should be colored. The game system, piano, and toy should be circled.

**page 124**

1. ant, mug, ruler, door
2. ant, ruler, mug, door

**page 128**

1. A
2. B
3. B
4. A

**page 129**

1. tudkehk(an)wtdeth
2. sr(use)qujezhpeib
3. wenbuxvd(each)nz
4. ainbn(said)kmipurw
5. dkipqug(there)eoha

**page 130**

1. rake
2. rat
3. top
4. hit
5. bike

**page 133**

1. 11
2. 13
3. 14
4. 18
5. 20
6. 15

**page 134**

1. 4
2. 1
3. 2 − 1 = 1
4. 3 − 3 = 0
5. Five objects should be drawn, and one of them should be crossed out.
6. Four objects should be drawn, and two of them should be crossed out.

**page 135**

There should be two green dresses and two red dresses drawn, for a total of four dresses.
Kiki has 2 red dresses.

**page 136**

There should be three red balloons, three yellow balloons, and three blue balloons drawn, for a total of 9 balloons.
There are 3 blue balloons.

**page 139**

1. cat; cap; camp
2. mop; stop; nod
3. sit; bit; lip

**page 143**

1. C
2. A
3. C
4. B

**page 144**

1. (How) can we fix this?
2. (She) is my friend.
3. (Their) play was good.
4. (Which) one is bigger?
5. Can you (do) it?

**page 145**

1. dimes
2. ants
3. cones
4. games
5. lakes

**page 146**

All words should be traced.

**page 148**

1. 9
2. 8
3. 6
4. 11
5. 5
6. 16

**page 149**

1. 5
2. 4
3. 2
4. Five fish should be drawn.

**page 150**

1. Student should have drawn 10 pancakes on the first plate, 3 pancakes on the second plate, and 5 pancakes on the third plate.
2. 10 + 3 + 5 = 18
3. There are 5 pancakes on the last plate.

**page 151**

Examples:

1. 

2. 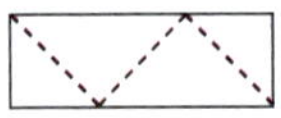

3. 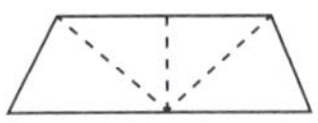

 

# Skills and Standards in This Book

Today's standards have created more consistency in how mathematics and English language arts are taught. In the past, states and school districts had their own standards for each grade level. However, what was taught at a specific grade in one location may have been taught at a different grade in another location. This made it difficult when students moved.

Today, many states and school districts have adopted new standards. This means that for the first time, there is greater consistency in what is being taught at each grade level, with the ultimate goal of getting students ready to be successful in college and in their careers.

## Standards Features

The overall goal for the standards is to better prepare students for life. Today's standards have several key features:

- They describe what students should know and be able to do at each grade level.
- They are rigorous and dive deeply into the content.
- They require higher-level thinking and analysis.
- They require students to explain and justify answers.
- They are aimed at making sure students are prepared for college and/or their future careers.

# Unit Outline

This book is designed to help your child meet today's rigorous standards. This section describes the standards-based skills covered in each unit of study.

|  |  | |
|---|---|---|
| Unit 1 | • Read simple, three-letter words.<br>• Practice reading and identifying high-frequency words.<br>• Use correct prepositions.<br>• Write a narrative about a picnic. | • Count up to 10.<br>• Draw pictures to solve word problems.<br>• Identify family members.<br>• Observe the weather over one day. |
| Unit 2 | • Read simple, three-letter words.<br>• Practice reading and writing high-frequency words.<br>• Identify and use capital letters.<br>• Write an informative text about police officers.<br>• Count up to 10. | • Identify flat shapes.<br>• Compare numbers to determine which is larger.<br>• Identify goods and services that community workers provide.<br>• Push, pull, and twist objects. |
| Unit 3 | • Read simple, three-letter words.<br>• Practice reading and writing high-frequency words.<br>• Determine how items are categorized.<br>• Write an opinion about a season.<br>• Count forward from a given number. | • Draw pictures to solve word problems.<br>• Identify what different community members have the authority to do.<br>• Use observable properties to identify a seed. |
| Unit 4 | • Read simple, three-letter words.<br>• Practice reading and identifying high-frequency words.<br>• Identify the opposites of common words.<br>• Write a narrative about spending time with friends. | • Compare groups to determine which group has more objects.<br>• Count up to 20.<br>• Identify attributes of solid shapes.<br>• Make a time line of a day.<br>• Observe how different objects move in different ways. |
| Unit 5 | • Read four-letter words with various blends.<br>• Practice reading and writing high-frequency words.<br>• Identify and use lowercase letters.<br>• Write an informative text about Earth's features. | • Count on to solve addition problems.<br>• Compare the sizes, weights, and capacities of objects.<br>• Identify natural features of Earth.<br>• Observe an animal. |



 

| | | |
|---|---|---|
| **Unit 6** | • Read and answer questions about a narrative.<br>• Practice reading and writing high-frequency words.<br>• Identify nouns.<br>• Write an opinion about pets.<br>• Add within 10. | • Identify attributes of flat and solid shapes.<br>• Draw pictures to solve word problems.<br>• Use calendars to identify a day, week, and month.<br>• Observe the weather over five days. |
| **Unit 7** | • Read and answer questions about a piece of nonfiction text.<br>• Practice reading and writing high-frequency words.<br>• Use correct punctuation.<br>• Write a narrative about a birthday party. | • Count up to 20.<br>• Subtract within 10.<br>• Draw pictures to solve word problems.<br>• Identify American symbols.<br>• Observe how objects roll. |
| **Unit 8** | • Read and answer questions about a narrative.<br>• Practice reading and writing high-frequency words.<br>• Identify verbs.<br>• Write an informative text about ducks.<br>• Create sets that are more than, less than, or equal to a given number. | • Use equations to represent addition and subtraction problems.<br>• Use pictures to solve word problems.<br>• Identify whether objects are short, long, light, or heavy.<br>• Identify needs and wants.<br>• Sort objects by observable properties. |
| **Unit 9** | • Read and answer questions about a piece of nonfiction text.<br>• Practice reading and identifying high-frequency words.<br>• Use correct spelling of simple words.<br>• Write an opinion about desserts.<br>• Count up to 20. | • Use number sentences to show addition and subtraction problems.<br>• Subtract within 10.<br>• Draw pictures to solve word problems.<br>• Identify what community helpers do.<br>• Identify what humans need to survive. |
| **Unit 10** | • Read and answer questions about a narrative.<br>• Practice reading and writing high-frequency words.<br>• Identify and use plural nouns.<br>• Write an informative text about washing your hands.<br>• Compare numbers to determine which number is larger. | • Subtract within 10.<br>• Draw pictures to solve word problems.<br>• Compose simple shapes to form larger shapes.<br>• Identify community landmarks.<br>• Describe the relative locations of objects. |

# Congratulations

______________________________!

*(name)*

**You have completed**

***Conquering Kindergarten!***

**presented on** ____________________

*(date)*

**Way to be a super scholar!**